SCHOLASTIC

ACTIVE™ Grammar

Practice Book 7

Rosemary Allen

Name ______________________________

Class ______________________________

Previously published as Grammar Skills 7 by Learners Publishing Pte Ltd.

First edition 2012
Reprinted 2012, 2013, 2014 (twice), 2015, 2016, 2017, 2018, 2019 (twice) , 2020, 2021, 2022, 2023, 2024, 2025

ISBN 978-81-8477-752-9

To Teachers and Parents

The study of English grammar in schools is changing as educators become increasingly aware of the important role context plays in language learning. The functional use of grammar has become a feature of English syllabuses around the world.

Active Grammar Practice Books have been written specifically to provide students with valuable links between basic, traditional grammatical concepts and the functional contexts in which they are used. The activities represent a blend of traditional and functional approaches to describe how texts 'work' in real-life situations and why certain grammatical choices are considered appropriate. Traditional grammar serves to provide students with the special terminology needed to talk about grammar, while functional grammar is intended to improve communicative competence by showing students how grammar works in the context of different text types.

The exercises in this book give students systematic guidance in developing an understanding of grammatical concepts. Panel notes are included to give hints for correct usage and highlight exceptions to grammar rules, as well as provide simple non-technical definitions to help students understand the exercises. The exercises incorporate learner-centred activities and are graded. Challenging ones are incorporated to motivate as well as interest the students.

It is hoped that teachers will find this series a valuable tool in their teaching programme, one that will provide students with a fascinating journey into the world of English language and a sound knowledge of how it works.

 ISBN 978-81-8477-752-9

Contents

	To Teachers and Parents	iii
Unit 1	Singular and Plural Nouns	1
Unit 2	Possessives	7
Unit 3	Indefinite Pronouns	13
Unit 4	Question Words	19
Unit 5	Helping Verbs	25
Unit 6	Modal Verbs	31
Unit 7	Present and Past Participles	36
Unit 8	The Present Perfect Tense	41
Unit 9	Degrees of Adjectives	47
Unit 10	Forming Adjectives from Nouns	53
Unit 11	Position of Adjectives	59
Unit 12	Types of Adverbs	65
Unit 13	Position of Adverbs	71
Unit 14	Prepositions	77
Unit 15	Transitional Devices	83
Unit 16	Punctuation and Capitalization	88
Unit 17	Affirmative and Negative Sentences	94
Unit 18	Imperative Sentences	101
Unit 19	Conditional Sentences	106
Unit 20	Active and Passive Voice	111
Unit 21	Direct and Indirect Speech	118
Answers		123

 ISBN 978-81-8477-752-9

1 Singular and Plural Nouns

Grammar Help

- You make most nouns plural by adding **s**. For example: *game – game**s**; zoo – zoo**s**; result – result**s**; correction – correction**s**.*
- If the noun ends with **s**, **x**, **sh** or **ch**, you make it plural by adding **es**. For example: *bus – bus**es**; fox – fox**es**; flash – flash**es**; sandwich – sandwich**es**.*
- Some nouns ending in **o** add **es** in the plural. For example: *hero – hero**es**; potato – potato**es***. Others simply add **s**. For example: *radio – radio**s**; piano – piano**s**.*
- If a noun ending in **y** has a consonant before the **y**, you change the **y** to **ies** in the plural. For example: *fly – fl**ies**, diary – diar**ies**, possibility – possibilit**ies**.*
- For most nouns ending in **fe**, and some nouns ending in **f**, you change the **f** to **v** to make a plural ending in **ves**. For example: *knife – kni**ves**, calf – cal**ves***. For others you simply add **s**. For example: *safe – safe**s**; handkerchief – handkerchief**s**.*

A ***Fill in the blanks in the following sentences with the correct plural form of the noun in brackets.***

1. I need some empty ____________________ to put these books in. (box)
2. Jane hates going to ____________________. (party)
3. Put the dirty ____________________ in the dishwasher. (plate)
4. There are seven ____________________ in a week. (day)
5. The men thanked us for saving their ____________________. (life)
6. Several ____________________ auditioned for the part of Queen Victoria. (actress)
7. Tom bought two ____________________ of bread at the baker's. (loaf)
8. Which of these ____________________ leads to the lake? (path)
9. A line of ____________________ marks the edge of the field. (tree)
10. The cook added some chopped ____________________ to the stew. (tomato)

 ISBN 978-81-8477-752-9

B ***Rewrite these sentences in the plural. You may need to change verbs and other words as well as nouns.***

1. This dish is cracked.

   ____

2. There was a fly in the soup.

   ____

3. A car is made in a factory.

   ____

4. The bird is building its nest.

   ____

5. Please put the book back on the shelf.

   ____

6. The girl made a video to send to her parents.

   ____

7. The street was full of traffic.

   ____

8. I bought a present for my friend.

   ____

9. The farmer had been ill-treating his donkey.

   ____

10. A dirty, ragged curtain covered the window.

    ____

 ISBN 978-81-8477-752-9

Grammar Help

- Some words have **irregular plural forms**. For example: *man – men, child – children, mouse – mice, foot – feet.*
- Many words of foreign origin have different rules for forming plurals. For example: *basis – bases, bacterium – bacteria, fungus – fungi, antenna – antennae, criterion – criteria.*
- Some nouns have the **same form in the singular and the plural**. For example: *one sheep – two sheep, an aircraft – several aircraft.*
- Some nouns that look plural are **always singular**. For example: *news, measles, athletics, mathematics.*
- Some plural nouns have **no singular form**. For example: *scissors, trousers, contents, clothes, cattle.*

C ***The box contains ten singular nouns and ten plural nouns. Write them in the correct columns below.***

apparatus	aquarium	cacti	camera	cattle
crisis	formula	gymnastics	houses	jeans
lice	media	news	phenomena	rabies
taxi	tooth	varieties	vertebrae	women

Singular		Plural	
____	____	____	____
____	____	____	____
____	____	____	____
____	____	____	____
____	____	____	____
____	____	____	____

Now give the singular forms of the plural words. If there is no singular form, put a cross (X) in that column.

Singular	Plural	Singular	Plural
____	____	____	____

 ISBN 978-81-8477-752-9

______	______	______	______
______	______	______	______
______	______	______	______
______	______	______	______

D ***Fill in the blanks in the following passage with the correct plural forms of the words in the box.***

bird	**child**	**crumb**	**father**	**fish**
flower	**foot**	**garden**	**gardener**	**goose**
hand	**leaf**	**man**	**mother**	**person**
plant	**rod**	**swan**	**swing**	**weed**

There were a number of ______ enjoying the sunshine in the park. Some ______ were playing on the ______, watched by their ______ and ______. Two ______ were sitting by the lake, with fishing ______ in their ______. However, they had not yet caught any ______. A little girl with bare ______ was paddling in the shallow water at the edge of the lake. She had a bag of ______, which she was throwing to the ______. There were several noisy ______ and a pair of ______ swimming gracefully along. The formal ______ on the other side of the park were looking beautiful. They contained many different ______ with colourful ______ and ______. A team of ______ kept everything neat and tidy: there were no ______ to be seen anywhere.

 ISBN 978-81-8477-752-9

Grammar Help

- A **compound noun** is made up of two or more words, which are sometimes joined to form a single word or linked by a hyphen. For example: *swimming pool, coffee cup, word-processor, sit-in, forget-me-not, toothbrush, flyover.*
- To make a compound noun plural, you usually add **s** (or **es**) to the second word. For example: *swimming pool**s**, coffee cup**s**, word-processor**s**, sit-in**s**, forget-me-not**s**, toothbrush**es**, flyover**s**.*
- However, if the first word is a noun but the second word is not, you make the first word plural instead. For example: *passer-by – passer**s**-by, brother-in-law – brother**s**-in-law, lady-in-waiting – lad**ies**-in-waiting.*

E ***Form ten compound nouns by taking one word from box A and one word from box B. Then make each compound noun plural.***

A: bench break class hair oil photo post runner screw wine

B: album bottle driver dryer in mark office painting room up

Singular	Plural	Singular	Plural

Now use each of these plural nouns in a sentence of your own.

1. ____________________
2. ____________________
3. ____________________

 ISBN 978-81-8477-752-9

4. ______

5. ______

6. ______

7. ______

8. ______

9. ______

10. ______

F ***The following passage contains twelve errors relating to singular and plural forms. Ten nouns and two verbs need to be changed. Put a ring round the incorrect words and write the correct forms on the lines below the passage.***

A deadly epidemic is sweeping the country. Several members of my family have had the disease: my sister, one of my son-in-laws and two of my grandchilds. Fortunately they have all recovered, but many others have not been so lucky. Persons listen to their radioes all day, anxious to find out if their lifes are at risk. The news are not good. The disease is caused by a bacteria that is resistant to all known antibiotics. It affects not only human beings, but also animals, especially cattle, which is an important source of income for many farmers. They cannot afford to lose their livestocks, or to fall ill themselves, so they are taking precaution to avoid carrying the germs from their fields into their houses on their foots or clothings. Scientists are working night and day to find a cure for the disease, or a vaccine that will control its spread. So far they have been unsuccessful.

______ ______ ______ ______

______ ______ ______ ______

______ ______ ______ ______

______ ______ ______ ______

 ISBN 978-81-8477-752-9

2 Possessives

Grammar Help

- You add **'s** to most singular nouns to show possession. For example: *the dog**'s** tail; Mary**'s** house; the princess**'s** servant.* (It is another way of writing phrases such as *the tail of the dog* or *the servant of the princess.*)
- You add an apostrophe alone to plural nouns that end in **s**. For example: *the boys**'** game; the dogs**'** ears.*
- However, you add **'s** to plural nouns that do not end in **s**. For example: *a children**'s** game; the mice**'s** ears.*
- You also sometimes add an apostrophe alone to long names ending in **s**. For example: *Archimedes**'** most famous discovery*. However, it would not be wrong to write *Archimedes**'s*** instead.
- For compound nouns and short noun phrases, you add **'s** to the last word. For example: *my sister-in-law**'s** friend; a passer-by**'s** help; the boy next door**'s** bike; Sue and Alice**'s** teacher.* (Notice the difference between the plural forms *sister**s**-in-law* and *passer**s**-by* and the possessive forms *sister-in-law**'s*** and *passer-by**'s***.)
- You can also use **'s** or **'** to talk about a length of time. For example: *a week**'s** work; four hours' delay.*

A ***Rewrite the sentences using possessive forms with 's or '.***

1. The surface of the road is uneven.

____

2. Today is the wedding anniversary of my parents.

____

3. The mother of Jenny is a doctor.

____

4. Birds eat the berries of the bush.

____

5. The bodice of the dress is torn.

____

 ISBN 978-81-8477-752-9

6. The queen needed the help of her lady-in-waiting.

____

7. I cannot find the lid of the box.

____

8. The teacher of the class is sick.

____

9. Sam gathered the eggs of the geese.

____

10. My sister goes to a school for girls.

____

B ***Write phrases containing possessive nouns to describe the following things or people. The first one has been done to help you.***

1. how hot the sun is — the sun's temperature
2. what men wear on their heads ______________
3. what the disease is called ______________
4. people travelling on a bus ______________
5. what my brother-in-law does for a living ______________
6. stopping work for a few minutes ______________
7. people that James likes to be with ______________
8. things used to row a boat ______________
9. the parts that bats use to fly ______________
10. a week spent away from home ______________

 ISBN 978-81-8477-752-9

C ***Write ten sentences of your own, each containing the possessive form of one of the words or phrases in the box.***

dog	Paul and Bill	passer-by	bus	workmen	five years
horses	waitresses	France	Uncle Jack and Aunt Mary		

Grammar Help

The words **my, mine, your, yours, his, her, hers, its, our, ours, their** and **theirs** are called **possessives**. They show who owns something.

- You use **my, your, his, her, its, our** and **their** before a noun. For example: ***my** bed; **her** best friend; **our** new house; **their** work.*
- You use **mine, yours, his, hers, ours** and **theirs** as pronouns in place of a noun phrase. For example: *These shoes are **yours**. **Mine** have white laces.* You can use possessive nouns on their own in a similar way. For example: *These shoes are **Tom's**. **Joe's** have white laces.*
- Remember that **its, yours, hers, ours** and **theirs** do not have an apostrophe, even though they show possession. The word **it's**, with an apostrophe, is a contraction of **it is** or **it has**.

 ISBN 978-81-8477-752-9

D ***Summarize each statement with a three-word sentence beginning with It is or They are and ending with a possessive pronoun. The first one has been done to help you.***

1. This scarf belongs to Jane. It is hers.
2. These drinks are for the boys. ____________
3. Mr Smith owns both those cars. ____________
4. These seats are for you and me. ____________
5. That is the book you lent me. ____________
6. My brother and I have a dog. ____________
7. Dad has bought a boat. ____________
8. Grandma gave me this necklace. ____________
9. Jack and Bill have received prizes. ____________
10. These are the flowers I gave Aunt Mary. ____________

E ***Fill in each blank with a possessive from the box. Use each word at least once.***

my mine your yours his her hers its our ours their theirs

Next month I am going to visit ____________ friend in England. ____________ name is Kate and she lives with ____________ family on the south coast. ____________ house is not far from the beach, so I will take ____________ swimsuit. However, I have heard that the English weather is not as warm as ____________, so I may not want to go swimming. Kate has told me not to bring any thick jumpers, as I can wear one of ____________ if I feel cold. She might also have to lend me some waterproof boots if it rains a lot (fortunately, ____________ feet are the same size).

 ISBN 978-81-8477-752-9

Kate's parents are richer than ________________: they have three cars and a boat. Some wealthy people do not like spending money, but Kate's parents are very generous with ________________, so I know they will treat me well. Mum and Dad have asked me to take plenty of photos. I do not have a camera, but ________________ brother says I can borrow ________________. Needless to say, he wants a favour from me in return. "________________ mobile phone is not working," he said. "I think ________________ battery has failed. Can I use ________________ while you are away? It probably won't work in England anyway." "OK," I said. "But don't expect me to pay for all ________________ phone calls!"

F ***Each of these sentences contains at least one error (sometimes more than one). Rewrite them correctly.***

1. There are two piano's in the hall.

   ____

2. Please give me you're phone number.

   ____

3. The shop does not sell womens shoes.

   ____

4. This is mine favourite film.

   ____

5. The twin's birthday is on the same day as my mothers'.

   ____

6. The patient had a good nights' sleep.

   ____

7. I lost my pen so Mary lent me one of his.

   ____

 ISBN 978-81-8477-752-9

8. The cat has eaten its dinner and now its licking it's paws.

____

9. Tom and Peter said the book was there's.

____

10. Your sisters' husbands are your brother's-in-laws.

____

11. Are you going to Nick's and Sues wedding?

____

12. He went to a boy's school where no students ever failed their exam's.

____

 ISBN 978-81-8477-752-9

3 Indefinite Pronouns

Grammar Help

You use an indefinite pronoun such as **someone** or **anything** when you are not talking about a particular person or thing.

- The indefinite pronouns **everything, something, anything** and **nothing** refer to things. For example: *There is **something** wrong with my computer. Can you see **anything**?*
- The indefinite pronouns **everyone, someone, anyone** and **no one** (or **everybody, somebody, anybody** and **nobody**) refer to people. For example: ***Everyone** laughed. **No one** knew the answer.*

A ***Fill in the blanks with everything, something, everyone or someone, using each one three times.***

1. I shall not begin until ______________ has stopped talking.
2. There is ______________ tickling my arm.
3. He thought he heard ______________ sneeze.
4. ______________ applauded at the end of the play.
5. I cannot fit ______________ into my suitcase.
6. Will ______________ please answer the phone.
7. ______________ must be done about this problem.
8. Listen carefully to ______________ the teacher says.
9. Jack knows ______________ who might be able to help us.
10. The house burned down and ______________ was destroyed.
11. If ______________ helps, the job will soon be done.
12. Can you lend me ______________ to write with?

 ISBN 978-81-8477-752-9

Grammar Help

- The indefinite pronouns **anything** and **anyone** are most often used in negative or interrogative sentences or questions. For example: *We do not need **anything** else. Is **anyone** there?*
- You use **nothing** and **no one** in negative statements and negative questions only. For example: *There was **nothing** left. Did **no one** see what happened?*
- Remember that you do not add **not** to the verb when you use **nothing** or **no one**. If you add **not** to the verb you must use **anything** or **anyone** instead. For example: *I know **nothing** about it. I do **not** know **anything** about it.*

B ***Rewrite these sentences using nothing and no one instead of anything and anyone.***

1. The doctor could not find anything wrong with the man.

   ____

2. She did not speak to anyone.

   ____

3. I do not have anything suitable to wear.

   ____

4. Won't anyone help us?

   ____

5. He has not done anything all morning.

   ____

6. Do not tell anyone your secret password.

   ____

7. Isn't there anything we can do?

   ____

8. Doesn't anyone care about these people?

   ____

 ISBN 978-81-8477-752-9

9. They have not had anything to eat.

10. I did not send anyone a postcard.

C ***Rewrite these sentences as questions containing* anything *and* anyone*. The first one has been done as an example.***

1. There is no one at the bus stop.
   Is there anyone at the bus stop?
2. They noticed nothing unusual.
3. Someone knows where she is hiding.
4. There was nothing in the cupboard.
5. He told someone what he had seen.
6. They have given her something to drink.
7. No one offered to help.
8. Something is wrong with this computer.
9. The police have arrested someone.
10. Nothing had changed in the village.

 ISBN 978-81-8477-752-9

Grammar Help

- You always use a singular verb when an indefinite pronoun is the subject. For example: *Nothing in this room* ***belongs*** *to me. Everyone* ***is*** *ready.*
- However, you can use **they**, **them**, **their**, etc. to refer back to the indefinite pronouns **everyone**, **someone**, **anyone** and **no one**. For example: ***Someone*** *has parked* ***their*** *car on our drive. If* ***anyone*** *phones, tell* ***them*** *I'll be back soon.* (In formal English you might use **he or she** instead of **they**, **his or her** instead of **their**, etc.)

D *Fill in each blank with* ***they, them, their, theirs*** *or* ***themselves.***

1. Someone was brushing ______________ teeth in the bathroom.
2. Everyone enjoyed ______________ at the party.
3. No one thought the book was ______________.
4. She never helps anyone with ______________ work.
5. When someone has flu, ______________ usually have a fever.
6. No one was helping ______________ to food, so I had to serve ______________.
7. Everyone ran as fast as ______________ could.
8. If anyone complains, give ______________ ______________ money back.
9. I cannot hang my coat on the peg because someone else has put ______________ there.
10. Tell everyone to bring a drink with ______________.

 ISBN 978-81-8477-752-9

E ***Fill in each blank with an indefinite pronoun from the box. Use each one only once.***

anyone	**anything**	**everyone**	**everything**
no one	**nothing**	**someone**	**something**

I was staying at my friend Sam's house overnight. After ______________ had gone to bed I heard a strange noise. It sounded like ______________ snoring in the room next door. At first I thought it might be Sam's father, but then I remembered that his parents' bedroom was on the other side of the house. The room next door was used as a study.

I sat up in bed and listened. "Is ______________ wrong?" asked Sam. "I thought I heard a snoring sound," I said. "There isn't ______________ in the room next door, is there?"

"No," replied Sam. "______________ has slept in there since Uncle Billy died. He was my grandfather's brother, and he came to live with us after his wife died. He used to sleep in that room, and he always kept ______________ to eat beside his bed in case he got hungry during the night. One night he choked on a nut. My parents rushed in to help him, but there was ______________ they could do. He died before the ambulance arrived. It was probably his ghost that you heard."

Terrified, I turned on the bedside light. Then I saw that Sam was laughing. He had made up the whole story just to frighten me. ______________ he had said was untrue. "So who is making that snoring sound?" I asked. Sam took me into the next room. There was his dog Jasper, fast asleep and snoring loudly.

 ISBN 978-81-8477-752-9

Now write eight sentences of your own, each containing one of these indefinite pronouns.

 ISBN 978-81-8477-752-9

4 Question Words

Grammar Help

The words we use to ask questions are sometimes called interrogatives or **wh**-words. They are **how, what, when, where, which, who, whom, whose** and **why**.

- The question words **what, which, who, whom** and **whose** are pronouns. For example: ***What*** *are you doing?* ***Who*** *told you that?* You can also use **what, which** and **whose** before a noun. For example: ***Which*** *picture do you prefer?* ***Whose*** *boots are those?*
- The question words **how, when, where** and **why** are adverbs. For example: ***How*** *do you know?* ***Where*** *is my camera?* You can also use **how** with another word. For example: ***How much*** *will it cost?* ***How far*** *did you go?*

A ***Fill in the blanks with the correct question words.***

Paul: ________________ did you get up so early?

Mum: I have a lot of work to do to prepare for our guests.

Paul: ________________ is coming?

Mum: Your father's old schoolfriend Peter is coming with his wife and two children. I told you about their visit days ago.

Paul: Sorry, I forgot. ________________ are they coming, and ________________ long for?

Mum: They should be here by five o'clock this afternoon, and they're staying until Monday.

Paul: ________________ are they all going to sleep?

Mum: Peter and his wife will sleep in the guest room. Their son can share your room and their daughter can share your sister's room.

 ISBN 978-81-8477-752-9

Paul: ______________ old is their son, and ______________ is his name?

Mum: He is called William and he is a year older than you. Instead of bothering me with all these questions, you could help me clear up this room. ______________ books are those?

Paul: ______________ ones?

Mum: The ones on the coffee table.

Paul: I think they're Dad's, but I'll tidy them away if you like. ______________ should I put them?

Mum: Take them up to our bedroom, and he can sort them out when he gets home from work.

Grammar Help

- The subject and verb in a question are usually inverted. That is, the subject comes after the verb, instead of before it. For example: *Where **is she**?*
- For verbs in the simple present and the simple past, you use the helping verb **do** in questions. You put the subject between **do/does/did** and the base form. For example: *How **does this machine** work? What **did he** say?*
- For verbs that already have a helping verb or modal verb, you put the subject after the first part of the verb. For example: *Why **should I** apologize? When **will the car** be repaired?*
- You do not invert the subject and verb if the question word is the subject. For example: ***Who ate** all the cookies? **What animal has** a long trunk?*

 ISBN 978-81-8477-752-9

B ***Write questions that invert the subject and verb of the given answers. The first one has been done to help you.***

1. What did he say?
   He said thank you.
2. ______________________________
   They will stay at their grandparents' house.
3. ______________________________
   The wedding is on 24th March.
4. ______________________________
   She looks like her sister.
5. ______________________________
   The door must be locked to keep burglars out.
6. ______________________________
   The patient is feeling much better.

C ***Complete the questions in any way that will match the given answers.***

1. How long ______________________________? Two hours.
2. Where ______________________________? To the post office.
3. Who ______________________________? I did.
4. What ______________________________? Four o'clock.
5. When ______________________________? In 1980.
6. Whose ______________________________? My sister's.
7. Where ______________________________? In the fridge.
8. Which ______________________________? The one on the table.
9. Why ______________________________? Because his bike has been stolen.
10. How ______________________________? You pull the handle towards you.

 ISBN 978-81-8477-752-9

Grammar Help

The question words **who**, **whom** and **whose** refer only to people, not to things.

- You can use **who** as a subject or as an object. For example: ***Who*** *broke this dish?* (subject) ***Who*** *did you meet at the party?* (object of verb) ***Who*** *is she talking to?* (object of preposition)
- In formal English you use **whom** instead of **who** as the object of a verb or preposition. For example: ***Whom*** *did you meet at the party? To* ***whom*** *is she talking?* (If you put the preposition before the question word, you must always use **whom** rather than **who**: you cannot say, "To who is she talking?")
- You use **whose** to ask about possession. For example: ***Whose*** *picture is the best?* ***Whose*** *are these shorts?*

D ***In the following sentences, is who the subject (S), the object of the verb (OV) or the object of a preposition (OP)? Write the correct letter or letters in the box.***

1. Who do you like best? ☐
2. Who took this photograph? ☐
3. Who is she going to the dance with? ☐
4. Who wants another cake? ☐
5. Who shall we invite to the party? ☐
6. Who did you send postcards to? ☐
7. Who can run the fastest? ☐
8. Who are these flowers for? ☐
9. Who will be chosen? ☐
10. Who will she marry? ☐

 ISBN 978-81-8477-752-9

E ***Fill in the blanks with who, whom or whose. If both who and whom can be used, write who(m).***

1. ______________ DVDs are those?
2. With ______________ did you travel home?
3. ______________ wrote the Harry Potter books?
4. ______________ did you tell?
5. ______________ idea was it?
6. ______________ is taller, Bill or Joe?
7. ______________ is the neatest handwriting?
8. From ______________ did you buy the camera?
9. ______________ has been elected president?
10. ______________ can we trust?

Grammar Help

You can use **what** or **which** before a noun to ask someone to make a choice. You use **what** if they can choose from an unlimited range of things. You use **which** if they must choose from a limited group of things. For example, if someone asks you, "***What*** *clothes should I take on holiday?*," they want you to suggest some suitable clothes. If they ask you, "***Which*** *clothes should I take on holiday?*," they want you to select some of the clothes they are showing you.

F ***Add What and Which to each pair of questions, then write a possible answer.***

1. ______________ books have you read lately? ______________________________

   ______________ books are for sale? ______________________________

2. ______________ tools should I use? ______________________________

   ______________ tools do we need, and where can we buy them? ______________

   ____

 ISBN 978-81-8477-752-9

3. ______________ animals are you drawing? ______________________________

______________ animals do they have on their farm? ______________________

4. ______________ colour shall I paint the walls? _________________________

______________ colour looks best: red or blue? ___________________________

5. ______________ time is the most convenient? ___________________________

______________ time does the bus leave? _________________________________

6. ______________ countries have you visited? ____________________________

______________ countries lie next to Pakistan? ___________________________

7. ______________ picture shall I paint? _________________________________

______________ picture did you paint? ___________________________________

8. ______________ words do you not understand? ___________________________

______________ words rhyme with “think”? ________________________________

 ISBN 978-81-8477-752-9

5 Helping Verbs

Grammar Help

Helping verbs (also called auxiliary verbs) are used with another verb to form a particular tense or voice, to make a sentence negative or interrogative, or to alter the meaning of the main verb.

- You use **be** as a helping verb with the present participle of the main verb to form the continuous tenses. For example: *The sun **is shining**. The men **were digging** a hole.* You can also use the helping verb **be** with a past participle to form the passive voice. For example: *The loaves **are baked** in a large oven. This house **was built** in 1956.*
- You use **have** as a helping verb with the past participle of the main verb to form the perfect tenses. For example: *I **have lost** my key. She thought she **had missed** the bus.*
- You use **do** as a helping verb with the base form of the main verb to form negative and interrogative sentences. For example: ***Does** this computer **work**? The train **did not stop**.*
- The other helping verbs are **will, shall, would, should, can, could, may, might, must, ought, need** and **dare**. They are called modal verbs. You use them with the base form of the main verb to express ability, possibility, permission, obligation, etc. For example: *Jack **can speak** four languages. It **might rain** this afternoon.*

A ***Fill in each blank with a helping verb from the box.***

am	is	are	has	have	do	does

1. The children ________________ playing in the garden.
2. This soup ________________ not taste very nice.
3. I ________________ wearing my new jeans.
4. James ________________ forgotten to bring his football boots.
5. ________________ all these books belong to you?
6. The furniture ________________ made of wood from the forest.

 ISBN 978-81-8477-752-9

7. ______________ you seen this film before?
8. The students ______________ not allowed to use mobile phones in class.
9. Alice ______________ promised to help us.
10. This bus ______________ not go to the town centre.
11. Mum ______________ washing her hair.
12. Where ______________ your grandparents live?
13. You ______________ made a few spelling mistakes.
14. I always do as I ______________ told.
15. ______________ you going to Paul's party?
16. What ______________ this word mean?
17. The phone ______________ not rung all day.
18. It ______________ snowing in England.
19. The police ______________ not think the man was murdered.
20. I ______________ put the apples in the fruit bowl.

B ***Circle all the helping verbs (including modal verbs) in the dialogue.***

Shop assistant:	Good morning. Can I help you?
Tom:	I hope so. I am looking for a present for my sister. I thought I might buy her a pair of gloves, but I do not know what size she takes. Perhaps she would like a handbag instead.
Shop assistant:	We have some lovely leather handbags here. They have just arrived from Italy. But they are rather expensive. How much were you planning to spend?
Tom:	I do not have a lot of money, but I may be able to borrow

 ISBN 978-81-8477-752-9

	some more from my father. He should be here in a few minutes. I left him trying to park the car.
Tom's father:	Hello, son. I finally managed to find a parking space. What have you bought for your sister?
Tom:	Nothing yet. There is a nice handbag here, but I need another thousand rupees. Could you possibly lend me some money?
Tom's father:	No, you must learn to spend only what you can afford.
Tom:	I was afraid you would say that. I shall go and look for a cheaper present somewhere else.

C ***Fill in the blanks with a helping verb and the correct form of one of the main verbs from the box.***

break build cure find forget grow scratch talk use wash

1. An adjective __________ __________ to describe a noun.
2. The cat __________ __________ you if you annoy it.
3. I __________ __________ Mary's phone number.
4. You __________ not __________ the school rules.
5. Most children __________ __________ by the age of three.
6. Why __________ birds __________ their nests in trees?
7. This medicine __________ __________ your cough.
8. Crops __________ __________ for food in most countries.
9. Sally __________ __________ her hair when the doorbell rang.
10. Michael is glad that he __________ __________ the missing book.

 ISBN 978-81-8477-752-9

D ***Rewrite these sentences, replacing* be *or* have *with a different modal verb each time. The first one has been done as an example.***

1. I have sent Grandma a postcard.

   I will send Grandma a postcard.

2. My little sister is writing her name.

   ______

3. He has apologized to his friend.

   ______

4. The students are working very hard.

   ______

5. She had forgotten to lock the door.

   ______

6. We were going to the cinema.

   ______

E ***Using* do, does *or* did *as a helping verb, write a question that could follow each statement. The first one has been done to help you.***

1. I have bruised my elbow.

   Does it hurt?

2. I saw a lovely necklace in the jeweller's shop.

   ______

3. We are going to stay with our cousins.

   Where ______

4. I have lent Bill my camera.

   ______

5. David gave Alice a bunch of flowers.

   ______

6. This device controls the temperature.

   How ______

 ISBN 978-81-8477-752-9

7. I am going to France for my holidays.

____

8. Sue is cooking the dinner.

____

9. My teacher asked me how old I was.

____

10. The card I sent Grandpa has not arrived yet.

When ____

Grammar Help

The verbs **be, have** and **do** can be used as main verbs as well as helping verbs. For example:

*My father **is** a lawyer.* (main verb)
*My father **is** baking a cake.* (helping verb)
*The children **have** no pets.* (main verb)
*The children **have** brushed their teeth.* (helping verb)
***Do** your homework.* (main verb)
***Do** not make a noise.* (helping verb)

The main verb **be** is usually followed by an adjective or a noun. The main verbs **have** and **do** are usually followed by a direct object.

F ***Find all the forms of be, have and do in the following sentences. Circle those that are main verbs and underline those that are helping verbs.***

1. My brother is afraid of the dark.
2. I have no idea what you are talking about.
3. Joe does the shopping and Sally cooks the food.
4. We saw a car being made at the factory.
5. These houses have been here for at least fifty years.
6. Do you know why the alarm is ringing?
7. Jane did not do her homework properly.

 ISBN 978-81-8477-752-9

8. They were having an argument about whose turn it was.
9. Have you had a phone call from Jack?
10. You are not being very helpful.
11. Mr and Mrs Wilson do not have any children.
12. I was watching Dad do the gardening.
13. The man who lives next door is a brain surgeon.
14. Do not be so mean!
15. She did not know what she was going to do.
16. I am learning how to play the guitar.
17. This is the most sensible thing he has ever done.
18. The winner will be given a prize.
19. We were being very careful not to do anything wrong.
20. It is not necessary to have a bath every day.

 ISBN 978-81-8477-752-9

6 Modal Verbs

Grammar Help

The modal verbs are **can, could, may, might, must, ought, shall, should, will** and **would**.

- You put most modal verbs before the base form of the main verb. However, you must add **to** between **ought** and the base form. For example: *You* ***should wear*** *a sunhat. You* ***ought to wear*** *a sunhat.*
- Modal verbs always have the same form. You cannot add **s, ed** or **ing** to a modal verb. However, you can use **could, might, would** and **should** as the past tense of **can, may, will** and **shall**. For example: *Jack* ***can*** *speak Spanish. Jack said he* ***could*** *speak Spanish.*

A ***Circle all the modal verbs in the following passage.***

You should look after your body — it has to last you a lifetime! There are many things you can do to stay fit and healthy. You must eat the right kinds of foods; otherwise you will become ill or overweight. A healthy diet contains plenty of fresh fruit and vegetables, and not too much sugar or fat. This does not mean you must never eat cakes or sweets — life would be very boring with no treats at all!

Exercise is also important. You ought to take a brisk walk several times a week. Busy people might find this rather difficult. However, there may be small ways in which you can alter your routine to include more physical activity. For example, if you travel to school or work by bus, you could get off one stop earlier and walk the rest of the way. Act now to avoid future health problems. Do not say "I shall change my lifestyle tomorrow" — do it today!

 ISBN 978-81-8477-752-9

Grammar Help

- You use **will** and **shall** to form the future tense. For example: ***Will*** *she be angry?*
- You use **can** and **could** to talk about ability. For example: *Sue* ***can*** *play the violin.*
- You use **can, could, may** and **might** to ask for permission. For example: ***May*** *we sit here?*
- You use **could, may** and **might** to talk about possibility. For example: *This* ***could*** *be the missing key.*
- You use **will** and **would** to make a request. For example: ***Would*** *you close the door, please?*
- You use **shall** and **should** to make a suggestion. For example: ***Shall*** *I open the window?*
- You use **should** and **ought** to say that something is advisable. For example: *He* ***should*** *apologize.*
- You use **must** to say that something is compulsory. For example: *You* ***must*** *obey the rules.*

B ***Choose the correct modal verb to fill in each blank.***

1. Please ______________ (may/shall) I borrow your pen?
2. Children ______________ (could/should) not be rude to their parents.
3. I thought it ______________ (will/would) be easy to sell my bike.
4. Owls ______________ (can/may) see well in the dark.
5. You ______________ (must/ought) not tell anyone this secret.
6. Mum ______________ (shall/will) be tired when she gets home.
7. The doctor was worried that the patient ______________ (may/might) not recover.
8. ______________ (Shall/Will) we go to the cinema instead?
9. Jack looked everywhere, but he ______________ (could/would) not find the missing sock.
10. The police ______________ (ought/should) to set a good example.
11. She asked if she ______________ (can/could) borrow my pen.
12. I promised that I ______________ (might/would) do my best.
13. They ______________ (can/may) not want to come with us.

 ISBN 978-81-8477-752-9

14. He ________________ (must/ought) to have told the truth.

15. We ________________ (shall/would) do the washing-up later.

16. The plants ________________ (might/must) be watered every day.

17. This box ________________ (ought/should) be big enough.

18. Do you think it ________________ (will/would) rain this afternoon?

C ***What might you say in the following situations? Write a sentence containing a modal verb for each. The first one has been done to help you.***

1. You are boasting about your swimming ability.
   I can swim ten lengths of the pool.

2. There are dark clouds in the sky.
   ____

3. You are thirsty.
   ____

4. Cycling is banned in the park.
   ____

5. You are helping your sister decide what to wear.
   ____

6. There is a cold draught in the room.
   ____

7. Your friend's mother is ill.
   ____

8. You have toothache.
   ____

9. Your brother has broken a valuable ornament.
   ____

10. You are explaining why you ran all the way to school.
    ____

 ISBN 978-81-8477-752-9

Grammar Help

The modal verb **would** has other uses.

- It can be used with **like** to make a polite offer or to say what you want. For example: ***Would*** *you* ***like*** *another cup of tea? I* ***would like*** *to go home.*
- It can be used with **rather** to state a preference. For example: *I* ***would rather*** *read a book than watch TV.*
- It can be used to talk about habitual actions in the past. For example: *Every morning she* ***would*** *take her dog for a walk.*

D ***Complete the responses to the questions in any way you choose.***

1. Would you like to go for a walk?

   I would rather ______________________________

2. Would you like a glass of lemonade?

   I would rather ______________________________

3. Would you like a game of chess?

   I would rather ______________________________

4. Would you like a pet dog?

   I would rather ______________________________

5. Would you like to travel around Europe?

   I would rather ______________________________

6. Would you like to be a doctor?

   I would rather ______________________________

7. Would you like to meet a famous writer?

   I would rather ______________________________

8. Would you like to live on a farm?

   I would rather ______________________________

9. Would you like a ride on my skateboard?

   I would rather ______________________________

 ISBN 978-81-8477-752-9

10. Would you like to sit here?

 I would rather ______________________________

Grammar Help

The verbs **need** and **dare** can be used as modal verbs or as lexical verbs (ordinary verbs with **s**, **ed** and **ing** forms).

- As modal verbs, they are followed by the base form of the main verb. For example: *Nobody* ***need know*** *about this. He is not sure whether he* ***dare tell*** *his parents.*
- When you use them as lexical verbs, you put **to** before the base form. For example: *Nobody* ***needs to know*** *about this. He is not sure whether he* ***dares to tell*** *his parents.*
- The lexical verb **need** can also be followed by a noun phrase or an **ing** form. For example: *I* ***need*** *some new shoes. The animals* ***needed*** *feeding.*

E ***In the following sentences, are need and dare used as modal verbs or as lexical verbs? Write M (for modal) or L (for lexical) in the box at the end.***

1. We need to find somewhere to stay. ☐
2. Does anyone need any help? ☐
3. I dare not open the box. ☐
4. Need you make so much noise? ☐
5. Few people dare to argue with her. ☐
6. You need not wait for me. ☐
7. How dare they treat us like that! ☐
8. These boots need cleaning. ☐
9. Dare you stroke a lion? ☐
10. She need never know what really happened. ☐

 ISBN 978-81-8477-752-9

7 Present and Past Participles

Grammar Help

The present participle is the **ing** form of a verb (*wearing, hoping, running*).

- To form the present participle of many verbs, you simply add **ing** to the base form. For example: *eat – eat**ing**, watch – watch**ing**, attack – attack**ing**, agree – agree**ing**.*
- However, if the verb ends in **e** with a consonant in front of it, you remove the **e** before you add **ing**. For example: *race – rac**ing**, manage – manag**ing**, operate – operat**ing**.*
- If the verb ends in **ie**, you change this ending to **y** before you add **ing**. For example: *die – **dying**, tie – **tying**.*
- If the verb ends in **consonant** + **vowel** + **consonant**, you usually double the final consonant before you add **ing**. For example: *rub – rub**bing**, strip – strip**ping**, model – model**ling**, refer – refer**ring**.*
- However, you never double **w** or **y**, and you do not double other consonants (except **l**) after an unstressed vowel. For example: *stay – stay**ing**, follow – follow**ing**, harden – harden**ing**, offer – offer**ing**.*

A *Write the present* **participle in the blank beside each verb.**

1. believe	________	11. pour	________
2. lie	________	12. rely	________
3. model	________	13. defend	________
4. gallop	________	14. open	________
5. groom	________	15. invent	________
6. spin	________	16. go	________
7. destroy	________	17. blossom	________
8. forget	________	18. grow	________
9. overlap	________	19. change	________
10 buzz	________	20. occur	________

 ISBN 978-81-8477-752-9

Grammar Help

You can use a present participle as follows:

- after **am, is** or **are** to form the present continuous tense. For example: *We **are waiting** for you.*
- after **was** or **were** to form the past continuous tense. For example: *The train **was leaving** the station.*
- as an adjective, or at the beginning of an adjectival phrase. For example: *a **leaking** roof; a boy **wearing** a baseball cap.*
- after verbs such as **hear** or **see**. For example: *I watched Dad **mowing** the lawn.*

B ***Complete the second sentence of each pair, using a different verb in the present continuous tense. The first one has been done to help you.***

1. The baby has woken up. Now it is crying.
2. Tom has washed the dishes. Now he ______________________________.
3. Mum has finished the housework. Now she ______________________________.
4. I have bought a present for Grandma. Now I ______________________________.
5. We have moved house. Now we ______________________________.
6. The rain has stopped. Now the sun ______________________________.
7. Jack has broken his model plane. Now he ______________________________.
8. The children have put their toys away. Now they ______________________________.
9. The plane has landed. Now the passengers ______________________________.
10. My brother has left school. Now he ______________________________.

C ***Fill in the blanks with present participles formed from the verbs in the box.***

burn	climb	die	fly	frighten	quarrel	ride	run	scamper	stand

1. The man ________________ by the door is my uncle.
2. Wash the vegetables in ________________ water.
3. Jack could smell something ________________.

 ISBN 978-81-8477-752-9

4. She told the children a ________________ story.

5. The planes ________________ over the house make a lot of noise.

6. Mary saw a mouse ________________ across the floor.

7. Ivy is a ________________ plant that grows up walls.

8. People ________________ bicycles are not allowed in the park.

9. I heard the children ________________ about the rules of the game.

10. He gave the ________________ soldier a drink of water.

Grammar Help

The past participle of **regular** verbs is the same as the simple past and ends in **ed** (*jumped, carried, banned*).

- To form the past participle of many regular verbs, you simply add **ed** (or just **d** if the verb already ends in **e**). For example: *blink – blink**ed**, close – close**d**.*
- If the verb ends in **y** with a consonant in front of it, you change the **y** to **i** before you add **ed**. For example: *try – tr**ied**, bully – bull**ied**.*
- If the verb ends in **consonant** + **vowel** + **consonant**, you usually double the final consonant before you add **ed**. For example: *rub – rub**bed**, strip – strip**ped**, model – model**led**, refer – refer**red**.*
- However, you never double **w** or **y**, and you do not double other consonants (except **l**) after an unstressed vowel. For example: *stay – stay**ed**, follow – follow**ed**, harden – harden**ed**, offer – offer**ed**.*

The past participle of **irregular** verbs does not end in **ed**. It is sometimes the same as the simple past (*got, held, said*), sometimes the same as the base form (*burst, cut, hit*) and sometimes different from both (*eaten, flown, rung*).

D ***Fill in all the blanks in the table.***

BASE FORM	PRESENT PARTICIPLE	PAST PARTICIPLE
________________	hoping	________________
________________	________________	dressed
catch	________________	________________

 ISBN 978-81-8477-752-9

__________	__________	rubbed
__________	burying	__________
__________	__________	drunk
see	__________	__________
__________	taking	__________
__________	__________	died
know	__________	__________
__________	__________	filled
__________	sweeping	__________
forget	__________	__________
swim	__________	__________
__________	having	__________

Grammar Help

You can use a past participle as follows:

- after **has** or **have** to form the present perfect tense. For example: *Mary **has finished** her homework. They **have promised** to help us.*
- after forms of the verb **be** in the passive voice. For example: *The main hall **is used** for public meetings. These photos **were taken** by my sister.*
- as an adjective, or at the beginning of an adjectival phrase. For example: *a **broken** window; electronic goods **made** in Japan.*

E ***Fill in each blank with the past participle of the given verb.***

1. The winner will be __________ (choose) by a panel of judges.
2. Joe has __________ (break) his leg.

 ISBN 978-81-8477-752-9

3. A ______________ (fall) tree blocked the road.
4. My boots are ______________ (cover) with mud.
5. Have you ______________ (meet) the president?
6. I am reading a book ______________ (write) by Charles Dickens.
7. Our new neighbours are a young ______________ (marry) couple.
8. All the soldiers were ______________ (give) medals.
9. Anna has not ______________ (brush) her teeth.
10. A picture ______________ (draw) by a five-year-old child won the competition.

F ***Circle all the present participles and underline all the past participles in the passage.***

Jack was sitting in the garden when he heard a strange noise coming from his neighbours' house next door. It was a loud buzzing sound, like the noise made by someone using a power tool. Jack knew that the house was empty. Mr and Mrs Brown, who lived there, were on holiday. They were staying with their relatives in England for several weeks.

Jack went indoors and told his mother about the strange noise. "I have also noticed some odd things lately," she said. "Yesterday I saw a man leaving the house. He was dressed in dirty jeans and an old T-shirt. I wonder if we should phone the police."

Just then, the doorbell rang. Jack opened the door and found the man described by his mother standing on the doorstep. "I am a friend of Mr and Mrs Brown's," he explained. "They have asked me to do some work in their kitchen while they are away. I hope the noise is not disturbing you." "Not at all," said Jack, glad that the mystery had been solved.

 ISBN 978-81-8477-752-9

8 The Present Perfect Tense

Grammar Help

The present perfect tense consists of **has** or **have** (the helping verb) followed by the past participle of the main verb. For example: *I **have forgotten**. The show **has begun**. Our visitors **have arrived**.*

- You use the present perfect tense to talk about past events that affect the present. For example: *I **have lost** her address so I cannot write to her.*
- You also use it to talk about a situation that began in the past and still exists. For example: *Uncle Jack **has worked** at the bank since he was sixteen years old.*

A. ***Choose the correct word to fill in each blank.***

1. Peter has ______________ (drawn/drew) a picture of his friend.
2. The cat has not ______________ (drank/drunk) its milk.
3. I have ______________ (taken/took) lots of photos with my new camera.
4. The phone has not ______________ (rang/rung) all morning.
5. Someone has ______________ (stolen/stole) my bike.
6. You have ______________ (did/done) a very foolish thing.
7. Our grandparents have ______________ (came/come) to live with us.
8. Sally has never ______________ (ridden/rode) a horse.
9. The house has ______________ (lain/lay) empty for several years.
10. Mum and Dad have ______________ (knew/known) Michael since he was a baby.
11. I have ______________ (forgot/forgotten) her brother's name.
12. Aunt Mary has ______________ (gave/given) me some good advice.
13. The ship has ______________ (sunk/sank).
14. Michael has ______________ (tore/torn) his new jeans.
15. Have you ever ______________ (driven/drove) a tractor before?
16. They have all ______________ (gone/went) home.

 ISBN 978-81-8477-752-9

B ***Fill in the blanks with the present perfect tense of the given verb.***

Everyone in the family __________ ______________ (make) a contribution to Grandma's 80th birthday party. Aunt Jane __________ ______________ (print) invitations on her computer. She __________ ______________ (send) them to all Grandma's relatives and friends. Uncle Bill __________ ______________ (lend) us lots of plates and glasses from his restaurant. He __________ ______________ (provide) some of the food and drink as well.

Mum __________ ______________ (bake) a large birthday cake. She __________ ______________ (cover) it with pink icing (Grandma's favourite colour) and __________ ______________ (write) "Happy 80th Birthday" across the top. Dad __________ ______________ (put) up decorations in the hall where the party is to be held this afternoon; my brother and I __________ ______________ (be) busy all morning blowing up balloons for this purpose. Other members of the family __________ ______________ (offer) to help with the clearing up after the party is over.

We __________ ______________ (share) the cost of the party among us. Some members of the family are richer than others, so they __________ ______________ (pay) more. But everyone __________ ______________ (do) the same amount of work to make the party a success. So far we __________ ______________ (manage) to keep it a surprise for Grandma. She knows nothing about it.

 ISBN 978-81-8477-752-9

C Fill in the blanks with the present perfect tense of a suitable verb.

1. Paul __________ ______________ his calculator. He cannot find it anywhere.
2. The rain __________ ______________. Let's go for a walk.
3. Dad __________ ______________ my bike, so I can ride it again.
4. We __________ ______________ our homework. May we watch TV now?
5. I __________ ______________ this film before, so I know how it ends.
6. Some men __________ ______________ the bank. The police are trying to catch them.
7. Kate __________ ______________ a competition, but she does not expect to win it.
8. I __________ ______________ my old computer at last. Now I can buy a new one.
9. The disease __________ ______________ throughout the community. Nearly everyone is infected.
10. You __________ ______________ my jacket by mistake. Please give it back to me.
11. Jane __________ ______________ me to her party, but I cannot go.
12. Someone __________ ______________ the window open. There is a cold draught.
13. The doorbell __________ ______________ the baby. It is crying.
14. Tom __________ ______________ his exam. His parents will be angry with him.
15. I __________ ______________ the instructions, but I do not understand them.
16. The teacher __________ ______________ our test papers. We will get the results tomorrow.
17. My baby brother __________ ______________ talking, but he can only say a few words.
18. I __________ ______________ the cake in two. You can have half each.

 ISBN 978-81-8477-752-9

Grammar Help

- You can use the present perfect tense with adverbs such as **just, already, never** and **yet**. For example: *Your postcard* ***has*** *just* ***arrived****. The children* ***have*** *already* ***gone*** *to bed.* Notice that you often put these words before the past participle.
- You do not use the present perfect tense with words and phrases such as **yesterday, last week, at four o'clock** and **two months ago**. You use the simple past instead. For example: *Your postcard* ***arrived*** *this morning. The children* ***went*** *to bed half an hour ago.*

D ***Write a response to the following commands. Use the word or phrase in brackets and the present perfect or simple past tense, as appropriate. The first one has been done to help you.***

1. Tell Mary your good news. (on Monday) I told her on Monday.
2. Open the window. (already) ______
3. Read this book. (last week) ______
4. Wash your hands. (just) ______
5. Feed the cat. (an hour ago) ______
6. Phone your aunt. (this morning) ______
7. Do your homework. (already) ______
8. Take your medicine. (at eight o'clock) ______
9. Lock the door. (just) ______
10. Post Grandma's birthday card. (yesterday) ______

E ***Fill in the blanks with the present perfect or simple past tense of the given verb.***

1. Everyone laughed when the clown ______ over. (fall)
2. I ______ in Pakistan since I was two years old. (live)
3. We ______ after the dog but we could not catch it. (run)
4. Dad ______ round the world when he was a young man. (travel)
5. Ask Mary if she ______ my car keys anywhere. (see)
6. My brother ______ me at chess several times before. (beat)

 ISBN 978-81-8477-752-9

7. Our visitors ______________ home two days ago. (go)
8. Jane has ______________ a new phone but she does not know how to use it. (buy)
9. The train ______________ at half past nine. (leave)
10. Tom ______________ his ankle, so he cannot play football. (break)
11. We cleared up the mess before Mum ______________ home. (come)
12. I do not know whether he ______________ his bike yet. (sell)
13. The pond ______________, so we can go skating. (freeze)
14. They ______________ dressed and went downstairs for breakfast. (get)
15. Hooray! The holidays ______________. (begin)
16. The building ______________ and several people were killed. (collapse)

Grammar Help

When you ask a question using the present perfect tense, you put the helping verb before the subject and the past participle after the subject. For example: ***Have*** *you* ***seen*** *Jack's new car?* ***Has*** *the plane* ***landed*** *yet?*

F ***Write questions in the present perfect tense to which the following answers could be given. The first one has been done to help you.***

1. Has the letter arrived?
   No, there was no mail this morning.
2. ______________________________
   No, I am afraid of flying.
3. ______________________________
   No, it is still at the station.
4. ______________________________
   Yes, they are ready for you to wear.
5. ______________________________
   Yes, you showed them to me yesterday.
6. ______________________________
   No, he is still eating it.

 ISBN 978-81-8477-752-9

7. ______________________________

Yes, you have missed the first few minutes.

8. ______________________________

No, they are still looking for her.

9. ______________________________

Yes, I saw one at the zoo.

10. ______________________________

Yes, it is working now.

11. ______________________________

Yes, I had it cut last week.

12. ______________________________

No, I don't think anyone wants to buy it.

 ISBN 978-81-8477-752-9

9 Degrees of Adjectives

Grammar Help

There are three **degrees** of adjectives: **positive** (*long, cold, new*), **comparative** (*longer, colder, newer*) and **superlative** (*longest, coldest, newest*).

- You use the positive degree with **as**. For example: *This jacket is not* ***as warm as*** *that one.*
- You use the comparative degree with **than**. For example: *Jack is* ***taller than*** *his brother.*
- You use the superlative degree with **the**. For example: *Our school is* ***the oldest*** *building in the village.* However, you use a comparative adjective with **the** when you are describing one of two people or things. For example: *Our school is the* ***larger*** *of the two buildings.*
- You sometimes have to change the ending of an adjective before adding **er** or **est**. For example: *pretty – prett**ier** – prett**iest**; safe – saf**er** – saf**est**; big – big**ger** – big**gest**.*

A ***Use the given adjective in the correct degree to fill in the blanks.***

1. This exercise is ______________ than the last one. (easy)
2. I used the ______________ piece of paper I could find. (thin)
3. They built a bridge at the ______________ part of the river. (wide)
4. The mountain is ______________ than all the surrounding hills. (high)
5. Your hair is not as ______________ as mine. (curly)
6. Paul was the ______________ of the twins. (brave)
7. They wished they were as ______________ as their friends. (rich)
8. I added some boiling water to make the tea ______________. (hot)
9. Mary is the ______________ person I know. (nice)
10. Dad has been much ______________ since he changed his job. (happy)

 ISBN 978-81-8477-752-9

B ***Rewrite the following sentences using a comparative or superlative adjective. There may be more than one correct answer. The first one has been done to help you.***

1. Joe is fourteen, Michael is twelve and Adam is ten.

   Adam is the youngest of the three boys.

2. Jane caught the 7:30 train and Sally caught the 8:30 train.

   Sally caught ________________________________.

3. I write more neatly than any of my classmates.

   My handwriting is the ________________________________.

4. This rock is not as heavy as that one.

   This rock is ________________________________.

5. Tom washed his hands but he did not wash his face.

   Tom's hands were ________________________________.

6. I chose a ring that cost less than all the others in the shop.

   The ring I chose was the ________________________________.

Grammar Help

- You use **er** and **est** to form the comparative and superlative of short adjectives. These include most one-syllable adjectives and some two-syllable adjectives. For example: *proud – proud**er** – proud**est**; narrow – narrow**er** – narrow**est**.*
- You use **more** and **most** to form the comparative and superlative of longer adjectives. For example: *anxious – **more** anxious – **most** anxious; comfortable – **more** comfortable – **most** comfortable.*
- Some adjectives have **irregular** comparative and superlative forms. For example: *good – better – best; bad – worse – worst.*

C ***Write the correct comparative or superlative form in the empty columns.***

POSITIVE	COMPARATIVE	POSITIVE	SUPERLATIVE
difficult	____________	shallow	____________

 ISBN 978-81-8477-752-9

sweet	______	hard	______
careful	______	bad	______
dirty	______	amazing	______
wet	______	fine	______
confident	______	obvious	______
good	______	simple	______
scared	______	adorable	______

D ***Fill in each blank in the following passage with one of the adjectives in the box, in its comparative or superlative form. Use each adjective only once, and use an equal number of comparative and superlative forms.***

cheap	**clever**	**expensive**	**good**	**healthy**	**delicious-looking**
high	**large**	**lazy**	**old**	**small**	**young**

Anna is the ______ student in her class. However, she is a tall girl, and many of her ______ classmates are ______ than her. She is not the ______ student, but she works hard, so she often earns ______ grades than some of the ______ boys and girls. At the end of last year she came first in almost all her exams. Her parents were so pleased that they took her out for tea to celebrate. They went to the ______ café in the town, and told Anna she could order whatever she wanted. Anna looked at the cakes on display. The ______ and ______ cake was also, needless to say, the ______. Anna's parents were not rich, so she chose one of the ______ cakes. This was also a ______ option, as the expensive cake was full of cream and covered with chocolate icing.

 ISBN 978-81-8477-752-9

Grammar Help

A **simile** is a phrase that uses **as** with an adjective and a noun to say what something is like. Here are some examples:

- *Her hair is* ***as white as snow****.*
- *The box is* ***as light as a feather****.*
- *Sally felt* ***as proud as a peacock****.*
- *The children were* ***as good as gold****.*
- *The water looked* ***as calm as a millpond****.*

Many similes are fixed phrases like these. However, you can also create new similes of your own to make your writing more interesting.

E ***Use the adjectives and nouns in the boxes to fill in the blanks in the similes.***

clear	cold	dead	free	high	pretty
quiet	slippery	solid	sour	tough	wise

a bat	a bee	coal	dust	a fox	a lion
a mule	an ox	a pancake	a rake	a razor	silk

as strong as ______________

as ______________ as a kite

as ______________ as a mouse

as black as ______________

as ______________ as leather

as blind as ______________

as busy as ______________

as ______________ as a dodo

as dry as ______________

as ______________ as a rock

as stubborn as ______________

as ______________ as vinegar

as ______________ as a picture

as smooth as ______________

as ______________ as crystal

as sharp as ______________

as brave as ______________

as ______________ as an eel

as cunning as ______________

as ______________ as ice

as flat as ______________

as ______________ as a bird

as ______________ as an owl

as thin as ______________

 ISBN 978-81-8477-752-9

Now use one of these similes to complete each of the following sentences.

1. Jane put on her new dress. She looked ______________________.
2. There are no hills in this part of the country. It is ______________________.
3. You can see the stones on the river bed. The water is ______________________.
4. Joe wished he had worn his gloves. His hands were ______________________.
5. My sister didn't say a word all afternoon. She was ______________________.
6. I haven't had time to read your letter. I have been ______________________.
7. Jack will help us move the piano. He is ______________________.
8. Nobody could chew the steak. It was ______________________.
9. You don't need to go on a diet. You are ______________________.
10. The animal had very dark eyes. They were ______________________.

F ***Complete the following sentences with any appropriate noun or noun phrase to create new similes of your own.***

1. The fruit tasted as sweet as ______________.
2. The little boy was as happy as ______________.
3. The surface felt as rough as ______________.
4. The traffic noise was as loud as ______________.
5. The baby bird was as fluffy as ______________.
6. The air smelt as pure as ______________.

Grammar Help

An ***absolute adjective*** is one that cannot have a comparative or superlative form. An example is the adjective ***perfect***: one thing cannot be more perfect than another, or made more perfect than it is – it is either perfect or not perfect.

 ISBN 978-81-8477-752-9

G ***There are ten absolute adjectives in the following passage. Circle each one.***

Dr Jackson was a keen collector of fossils. He had travelled all over the world and had found many interesting specimens. There were hundreds of fossils in his collection, and each was unique. They ranged from the tiny remains of sea creatures to huge bones from extinct dinosaurs. Dr Jackson's interest in fossils had begun as a young boy, when he found a perfect ammonite on the beach. Looking more carefully at the rocks and stones around him, he discovered several more. When he returned home he made a case to display his fossils, using an empty box and a square piece of glass that he found in his father's workshop. People used to ask Dr Jackson if he would stop searching when his collection was complete. He said that was impossible, because there was an infinite number of fossils in the world. He would continue searching until he was too old and weak to travel. Unfortunately, on his final trip to Africa, he contracted a fatal illness and died soon after his return.

Now match the absolute adjectives you have found with their definitions.

1. ______________ with four equal sides
2. ______________ causing death
3. ______________ last
4. ______________ that cannot be done
5. ______________ containing nothing
6. ______________ being the only one of its kind
7. ______________ with no faults or flaws
8. ______________ no longer living anywhere
9. ______________ having no end or limit
10. ______________ with nothing missing

 ISBN 978-81-8477-752-9

10 Forming Adjectives from Nouns

Grammar Help

You can add various endings to nouns to change them into adjectives.

- The endings **ful**, **ous**, **y** and **ed** form adjectives that mean "having this quality or thing". For example: *a **successful** mission; a **dangerous** activity; a **healthy** diet; a **bearded** man.*
- The ending **less** forms adjectives that mean "not having this quality or thing". For example: *a **painless** operation; **homeless** people.*
- The endings **al** and **ary** form adjectives that mean "of this thing". For example: *a **national** flag; a **legendary** hero.*
- The endings **ic**, **ish** and **ly** form adjectives that mean "of or like this person or thing". For example: *an **artistic** child; a **boyish** smile; a **neighbourly** gesture.* The ending **ly** can also mean "having this quality" or "happening once in this period of time". For example: *a **costly** ring; a **weekly** magazine.*
- Other endings that can change nouns into adjectives are **some** and **able**. For example: *an **awesome** achievement; **fashionable** clothes.*

A ***Choose the correct ending to form a suitable adjective from the given noun.***

1. Alice is a very talent__________ (ary, ed, ful) musician.
2. That was a rather fool__________ (ful, ic, ish) thing to do.
3. Everyone was compliment__________ (ary, ly, y) about my painting.
4. This website contains some help__________ (able, ful, less) information.
5. They live in a mountain__________ (ed, ic, ous) region of the country.
6. You have made a number of care__________ (ful, ish, less) mistakes.
7. He gave her a brother__________ (less, ly, y) hug.
8. The shop sells books and education__________ (al, ary, ic) toys.
9. A patriot__________ (ary, ic, ly) person would never betray their country.
10. Go and wash your dirt__________ (ful, ly, y) hands.

 ISBN 978-81-8477-752-9

B ***The twelve adjectives in the box have the wrong endings. Rewrite them correctly on the lines below, so that each noun and ending appears only once.***

coasted	troubleless	delightic
customable	wheely	poisonary
hopely	selfsome	friendal
knowledgeful	heroish	stormous

______________ ______________ ______________

______________ ______________ ______________

______________ ______________ ______________

______________ ______________ ______________

Grammar Help

You sometimes have to make a spelling change when you add these endings.

- If the noun ends in **y** with a consonant in front of it, you change this to **i** before adding **ful, ous, less**. For example: *beauty* → *beauti**ful**, glory* → *glor**ious**, pity* → *piti**less***. Before **al** and **ic** you remove the **y**. For example *navy* → *nav**al**, botany* → *botan**ic***.
- Some nouns ending in **y** form adjectives ending in **ical**. For example: *biology* → *biolog**ical***. Often the adjective can end in **ic** or **ical**, sometimes with slightly different meanings. For example: *geometry* → *geometr**ic*** or *geometr**ical**, economy* → *econom**ic*** or *econom**ical***.
- If the noun ends in ***e*** with a consonant in front of it, you remove the ***e*** before adding **al**, **ic**, **ish**, **ous** or **y**. For example: *globe* → *glob**al**, scene* → *scen**ic**, style* → *styl**ish**, nerve* → *nerv**ous**, stone* → *ston**y***
- If the noun ends in **consonant** + **vowel** + **consonant** (except **w**) you double the final consonant before adding **y** or **ish**. For example: *fog* → *fo**ggy**, star* → *sta**rry**, man* → *man**nish*** but *snow* → *snow**y***.
- If the noun ends in ***ce***, you usually change this to **ti** before adding **al**. For example: *spa**ce*** → *spa**tial**, essen**ce*** → *essen**tial***. But note the exception *ra**ce*** → *ra**cial***.

 ISBN 978-81-8477-752-9

- If the noun ends in **our**, you change this to **or** before adding **ous**. For example: *glam**our** → glam**orous**.*
- Some nouns ending in **le** form adjectives ending in **ular**. For example: *ang**le** → ang**ular**, circ**le** → circ**ular**.*
- Some changes do not follow a particular rule. For example: *skill → skil**ful*** (the noun loses an **l**), *day → dai**ly*** (the **y** changes to **i**), *space → spaci**ous*** (the **e** changes to **i**), *mischief → mischiev**ous*** (the **f** changes to **v**).

C1. ***Write the adjective formed from the given noun and ending, then use it to describe another noun. The first one has been done as an example.***

1. mud + y = muddy ______ a muddy path ______
2. triangle + ar = ______ ______
3. residence + al = ______ ______
4. pity + ful = ______ ______
5. victory + ous = ______ ______
6. juice + y = ______ ______
7. majesty + ic = ______ ______
8. humour + ous = ______ ______
9. nature + al = ______ ______
10. peace + ful = ______ ______
11. fun + y = ______ ______
12. space + ous = ______ ______
13. base + ic = ______ ______
14. wave + y = ______ ______
15. adventure + ous = ______ ______
16. parent + al = ______ ______
17. snob + ish = ______ ______
18. cloud + y = ______ ______
19. poison + ous = ______ ______

 ISBN 978-81-8477-752-9

20. navy + al = ______________ ______________________

C2. ***Now use ten of the phrases you have created in sentences of your own.***

____

____

____

____

____

____

____

____

____

____

D ***Fill in the blanks with adjectives formed from the nouns in the box.***

music	wonder	spectacle	sun	botany	acrobat
hour	cloud	fame	recreation	skill	colour
rain	need	rectangle	tradition	leisure	muscle

It was a fine, ______________ day. Jane looked out of the window at the ______________ blue sky and smiled. She and her sister were going to an open-air show at the park, and it might have been cancelled if the weather had been ______________. There was an ______________ bus service from the end of their street to the park, which would get them there thirty minutes before or after the start of the show. ______________ to say, they caught the early bus. This gave them time for a ______________ stroll through the ______________ garden

 ISBN 978-81-8477-752-9

on the way to the ________________ area, where a ________________ stage had been set up in the middle of the field.

They had a ________________ time at the show. There were performers there from all over the world, some of them quite ________________ in their own countries. Wearing ________________ costumes, they performed ________________ dances to tunes played on unusual ________________ instruments. The most ________________ part of the show was the ________________ display. The acrobats' ________________ legs and arms enabled them to jump high into the air and walk across the stage on their hands. Jane's favourite performer was a conjurer, whose ________________ magic tricks made the audience gasp with amazement.

Grammar Help

You can also use some nouns like adjectives before other nouns. For example: *There is a stain on the* ***lounge*** *carpet. They have a* ***swimming*** *pool in their garden.*

E ***Using one of the nouns in the given phrase as an adjective before the other, write a sentence containing the new phrase. The first one has been done as an example.***

1. a teacher of science — Our **science teacher** is good at explaining things.
2. bowls for soup ________________
3. an invitation to a wedding ________________
4. the curtains in the bathroom ________________
5. a book about cookery ________________
6. uniform worn for school ________________

 ISBN 978-81-8477-752-9

7. the door of the garage ________________

8. my ticket for the train ________________

9. a market selling fish ________________

10. hairs from a dog ________________

 ISBN 978-81-8477-752-9

11 Position of Adjectives

Grammar Help

Adjectives can come in three different positions.

- They most often come immediately before a noun. This is the **attributive** position. For example: *He drives a* ***red*** *car. She brushed her* ***curly*** *hair.*
- They occasionally come immediately after a noun or pronoun. This is the **postpositive** position. For example: *I will speak to the people* ***concerned****. Do you have anything* ***important*** *to say?*
- They sometimes come after a verb such as **be, become, look** or **sound**. This is the **predicative** position. *I feel* ***sick****. The cake tasted* ***delicious****.*

A ***Are the adjectives in bold print in the attributive (A), postpositive (Po) or predicative (Pr) position? Write the correct letter or letters in the box.***

1. Alice was wearing her **new** dress. ☐
2. Those flowers smell **lovely**. ☐
3. There are some **clean** towels in the cupboard. ☐
4. Please give me something **easier** to do. ☐
5. It goes **dark** at about five o'clock. ☐
6. This bag feels **heavier** than that one. ☐
7. The children **involved** were praised for their bravery. ☐
8. The building is guarded by a **fierce** dog. ☐
9. The supermarket is not **open** yet. ☐
10. All those **present** voted in favour of the plan. ☐

 ISBN 978-81-8477-752-9

B ***Underline the adjectives in this letter and put a ring round the noun or pronoun they describe. (You can ignore the word Dear at the beginning and any nouns used like adjectives before another noun.)***

Dear Mum and Dad

I am having a great time at the adventure camp. Our instructor, whose name is Joe, is a nice man, but he is also rather strict. Yesterday he took us to the forest and gave us a difficult task to do. Working in small groups, we had to build huts using only the materials available, such as branches, dead leaves and mud. Joe said that the huts must be waterproof, but he did not tell us why. We later found out that we would have to sleep in them overnight, and the weather forecast said there might be heavy rain. When our hut was ready, we had to find something suitable to sleep on. I gathered some dry ferns for my bed. They smelt lovely. When I lay down my bed felt quite soft, but the ground below was hard and I did not have a comfortable night. Tomorrow we are going sailing on the lake. I hope we will not have to make the boats!

Love

David

Now list the adjectives from the passage in the correct columns below.

Attributive	Postpositive	Predicative
____________	____________	____________
____________	____________	____________
____________	____________	____________
____________	____________	____________

 ISBN 978-81-8477-752-9

Grammar Help

- Many adjectives can be used in all three positions. For example: *It was a **hot** day. I would like something **hot** to drink. The water felt **hot**.*
- However, some cannot be used in the attributive position. They include **afraid**, **alive**, **asleep**, **awake** and **ready**. For example, you can say, "*The boy is **afraid**,*" but you cannot say, "*The **afraid** boy*".
- Nouns used as adjectives can only come in the attributive position, directly before the noun. For example, you can say, "*These are **coffee** cups,*" but you cannot say, "*These cups are **coffee***".

C ***For each adjective, tick one or both boxes, then write a short sentence using the word correctly.***

	Attributive	Predicative	
1. old			
2. asleep			
3. sweet			
4. sad			
5. school			
6. dangerous			
7. alive			
8. narrow			

 ISBN 978-81-8477-752-9

9. black [ ] [ ] ______________________________

10. history [ ] [ ] ______________________________

D ***Change the order of the words to make a sentence and write it with the correct punctuation on the line below.***

1. felt cold water the

____

2. computer new sally a has

____

3. rather seemed the upset woman

____

4. that necklace gave who you gold

____

5. interview for wear smart your something

____

6. the window entered the through open burglar

____

7. yet her Mum has car found keys

____

8. on the plates shelf are the dinner top

____

9. awake the were parents children before excited their

____

10. ornament you lovely that china where buy did

____

 ISBN 978-81-8477-752-9

Grammar Help

You can use more than one adjective to describe a noun.

- In the attributive position, you usually write the adjectives in a string, sometimes with commas between them. For example: *She has **long black** hair. He is a **polite, friendly, popular** boy.*
- You most often use commas between attributive adjectives when they are all adjectives of quality, as in the second example above. You should not put a comma before the noun, or before a noun being used as an adjective. For example, you must write *our **new science** teacher* (not *our **new, science** teacher*).
- You must put **and** between attributive adjectives of colour. For example: *There was a **pink and grey** rug on the floor.*
- You also use **and** when two or more adjectives are in the predicative position. For example: *Her hair is **long and black**. The boy is **polite, friendly and popular**.* You must always put a comma after the first of three predicative adjectives.

E ***Change the position of the adjectives from attributive to predicative, or from predicative to attributive. The first one has been done to help you.***

1. We have a difficult, dangerous mission.

   Our mission is difficult and dangerous.

2. The mouse's eyes are small and round.

   The mouse has ____________ eyes.

3. Uncle Jack has a loud deep voice.

   Uncle Jack's voice is ____________.

4. We watched a film that was long and boring.

   We watched a ____________ film.

5. It was a cold, wet, windy day.

   The weather was ____________.

6. The insect's body is black and yellow.

   The insect has a ____________ body.

7. I picked up a stone that was small, smooth and white.

   I picked up a ____________ stone.

 ISBN 978-81-8477-752-9

8. She makes delicious creamy tomato soup.

   Her tomato soup is ________________.

9. These glass bowls are fragile, so be careful with them.

   Be careful with these ________________ bowls.

10. The British flag is red, white and blue.

    Britain has a ________________ flag.

 ISBN 978-81-8477-752-9

12 Types of Adverbs

Grammar Help

There are several different types of adverbs, such as adverbs of manner, time, frequency, place and degree.

- Adverbs of **manner** tell you **how** the action of a verb is performed. They are often formed by adding **ly** to an adjective. For example: *We sailed **slowly** across the bay. The children played **happily** together. She stroked the cat **gently**.*
- Notice that you sometimes change the ending of the adjective before adding **ly**. You change **y** to **i** (as in *noisy* → *noisi**ly***). You remove the final ***e*** of adjectives that end in **ble**, **ple**, **tle**, etc. (as in *sim**ple*** → *sim**ply***). You add **ally** to adjectives that end in **ic** (as in *enthusiast**ic*** → *enthusiastic**ally***).
- Some adverbs of manner (such as **fast** and **hard**) do not end in **ly**. Remember that **well** is the adverb corresponding to the adjective ***good***.

A ***Fill in the blanks with adverbs of manner formed from the adjectives in the box.***

accidental	**blind**	**careful**	**deliberate**	**greedy**	**loud**
proper	**quick**	**quiet**	**sleepy**	**sudden**	**thirsty**

Kate woke up in the middle of the night feeling thirsty. She did not want to disturb her sister, who slept in the same room, by switching the light on. Reaching ________________ in the dark for the glass of water on her bedside table, she ________________ knocked it over. She ________________ got out of bed and mopped up the spilt water with some tissues. "What's going on?" asked her sister ________________. Kate explained. "I'm going down to the kitchen to get another drink," she added.

 ISBN 978-81-8477-752-9

Carrying her empty glass, she tiptoed ____________ out of the room and went downstairs. As she entered the kitchen her cat greeted her, miaowing ____________. "Hush!" said Kate. "You'll wake everybody up." Taking a bottle of milk from the fridge, she poured some into the cat's bowl. It stopped miaowing and lapped up the milk ____________. Kate filled her glass with water and ____________ carried it back upstairs. As she reached the top, she ____________ remembered that she had forgotten to put the milk back in the fridge. She was not even sure if she had put the lid back on the bottle ____________.

She hadn't. The cat had leapt onto the table, knocking the bottle over, and when Kate reached the kitchen it was ____________ drinking the spilt milk. "You did that ____________, didn't you?" she said. The cat purred.

B ***Rewrite these sentences using an adverb of manner corresponding to the adjective in bold print. The first one has been done to help you.***

1. James has **neat** handwriting.

   James writes neatly.

2. Grandma is a very **careful** driver.

   ____

3. The chef cut the meat into **thin** slices.

   ____

4. There was **heavy** rain yesterday.

   ____

5. This is the **slow** train.

   ____

 ISBN 978-81-8477-752-9

6. I am a **good** pianist.

____

Grammar Help

- Adverbs of **time** tell you **when** the action of a verb is performed. They include **soon**, **already**, **yesterday** and **tomorrow**. For example: *I have not bought my ticket* ***yet****. They left ten minutes* ***ago****.* Some adverbs of time are made up of two words, such as **next week** or **yesterday morning**.
- Adverbs of **frequency** tell you **how often** the action of a verb is performed. They include **sometimes**, **never**, **fortnightly**, **every day** and **once a week**. For example: *She* ***always*** *forgets my name. The festival is held* ***annually****.*

C ***Write ten sentences about yourself using the given adverbs of time and frequency.***

1. I always ______________________________
2. Yesterday evening I ______________________________
3. I never ______________________________
4. I usually ______________________________
5. I ______________________________ next year.
6. I often ______________________________
7. On Friday I ______________________________
8. I sometimes ______________________________
9. I ______________________________ tomorrow.
10. I ______________________________ ago.
11. I rarely ______________________________
12. I ______________________________ last week.

 ISBN 978-81-8477-752-9

Grammar Help

- Adverbs of **place** tell you **where** the action of a verb is performed: its position or direction. They include **here, outside, off** and **away**. For example: *They looked* ***everywhere*** *for the missing dog. A large truck drove* ***past.***
- Adverbs of **degree** tell you **how much**. They include **rather, quite, very** and **hard**. You can use them with verbs, adjectives or other adverbs. For example: *I* ***strongly*** *disapprove of such behaviour. This question is* ***extremely*** *difficult. You are walking* ***too*** *quickly.*

D ***Fill in the blanks with pairs of adverbs that mean the opposite of each other. Do not use the same pair more than once.***

1. The students stood ________________ when the principal entered, then they sat ________________ again.
2. I switched ________________ the main light and switched ________________ my bedside lamp.
3. The garage already has two cars ________________, so you will have to leave yours ________________.
4. She told them to leave, so they went ________________ and never came ________________.
5. In most houses the bathroom is ________________ and the kitchen is ________________.
6. The sun came ________________ for a while, then it went ________________ again.
7. I live in an apartment block. One of my friends lives on the floor ________________ and another lives on the floor ________________.
8. My seat is ________________ and yours is ________________, on the opposite side of the table.
9. There are reduced rates for adults aged 60 or ________________ and for children aged 12 or ________________.
10. Football is usually played ________________ and badminton is usually played ________________.

 ISBN 978-81-8477-752-9

E ***What might you say in the following situations? Write your statements on the lines below, each containing a different adverb of degree from the box. The first one has been done to help you.***

considerably	**exceptionally**	**extremely**	**quite**	**rather**
reasonably	**really**	**slightly**	**too**	**very**

1. You like Anna's new hairstyle.
   Anna's hair looks really nice.
2. Your old house was tiny and your new house is huge.
   ____
3. The sea is not warm enough to swim in.
   ____
4. Your father is 40 and your mother is 39.
   ____
5. Tom paints beautiful pictures.
   ____
6. You cannot solve a puzzle.
   ____
7. You know for certain that you locked the door.
   ____
8. The team played much better than usual.
   ____
9. Your feet hurt, but not badly.
   ____
10. You scored 70% in the test.
   ____

 ISBN 978-81-8477-752-9

F ***List the adverbs in the box under the correct headings below.***

aboard	**back**	**carelessly**	**clearly**	**down**
eagerly	**fast**	**every week**	**finally**	**highly**
hourly	**later**	**last night**	**much**	**often**
once a month	**out**	**somewhere**	**rarely**	**slightly**
this afternoon	**so**	**still**	**very**	**well**

Manner	Time	Frequency	Place	Degree
____________	____________	____________	____________	____________
____________	____________	____________	____________	____________
____________	____________	____________	____________	____________
____________	____________	____________	____________	____________
____________	____________	____________	____________	____________

 ISBN 978-81-8477-752-9

13 Position of Adverbs

Grammar Help

You can put adverbs in various parts of the sentence. The position depends on what kind of adverb it is, and how important it is.

- You can put most adverbs after the verb, or after its object if it has one. This is called the **end position**. For example: *He walked **slowly** up the hill. I bought this book **yesterday**. Please take your muddy boots **off**. The fire destroyed the hotel **completely**.*
- You can put many adverbs before the verb, to add emphasis. This is called the **mid position**. For example: *He **slowly** walked up the hill. I **often** buy books.* If the main verb has a helping verb, you put the adverb between the helping verb and the main verb. For example: *She was **gently** stroking the cat. The fire has **completely** destroyed the hotel.*
- You can put some adverbs at the beginning of a sentence, for greater emphasis. This is called the **initial position**. For example: ***Suddenly** the balloon burst. **Soon** it will be daylight. **Away** they ran.* The initial position is most often used in narratives.

A ***Are the adverbs in bold print in the end (E), mid (M) or initial (I) position? Write the correct letter in the box.***

1. Dad **sometimes** helps me with my homework. ☐
2. **Cautiously** she stepped aboard the boat. ☐
3. I have **never** seen this film before. ☐
4. First you must switch the computer **on**. ☐
5. **Tomorrow** we are going to the seaside. ☐
6. Sally ran **upstairs** to fetch her camera. ☐
7. He **fortunately** remembered to close the window. ☐
8. I tied the rope **securely** to the tree. ☐

 ISBN 978-81-8477-752-9

9. **Off** they went to search for the treasure.

10. The train **suddenly** stopped.

Grammar Help

- **Adverbs of manner** that end in **ly** usually come in the end position or the mid position, but some can also come in the initial position. For example: *She washed the vase **carefully**. She **carefully** washed the vase. **Carefully** she washed the vase.*
- Adverbs of manner that do not end in **ly** can only come in the end position. For example: *You have done your homework **well**. I can run **fast**.*

B ***Rewrite these sentences, moving the adverbs from the mid position to the end position, or from the initial position to the mid position.***

1. The children were happily playing in the garden.

   ____

2. Gradually the weather became warmer.

   ____

3. He playfully pulled his sister's hair.

   ____

4. Hungrily they devoured the food.

   ____

5. The branches were gracefully swaying in the breeze.

   ____

6. Sally deliberately dropped the ball.

   ____

7. Reluctantly he left the shop without buying anything.

   ____

 ISBN 978-81-8477-752-9

8. I hastily ran to the bus stop.

____

9. Secretly she was hoping that the show would be cancelled.

____

10. I politely asked the boys to make less noise.

____

Grammar Help

- Some one-word **adverbs of time and frequency** are most often used in the mid position. For example: *They have **finally** finished mending the road. You **never** listen to what I say.*
- Some are most often used in the end position. For example: *I will help you **later**. The workers are paid **weekly**.*
- Others can come in any position. For example: *It will be dark **soon**. It will **soon** be dark. **Soon** it will be dark. **Sometimes** I go by bus. We **sometimes** have pizza for lunch. He wears glasses **sometimes**.*
- Two-word adverbs of time and frequency can come in the end position or the initial position, but not in the mid position. For example: *She has a shower **every morning**. **Last year** we went to India.*

C ***Write sentences of your own containing the adverb in brackets in the given position.***

1. (**rarely**; mid position) ______________________
2. (**this afternoon**; end position) ______________________
3. (**yesterday**; initial position) ______________________
4. (**quietly**; mid position) ______________________
5. (**ago**; end position) ______________________
6. (**sometimes**; initial position) ______________________
7. (**never**; mid position) ______________________
8. (**sadly**; end position) ______________________
9. (**frequently**; mid position) ______________________

 ISBN 978-81-8477-752-9

10. (**fortunately**; initial position) ______________________________

Grammar Help

- **Adverbs of place** usually come in the end position. For example: *We have lived **here** for five years. I threw the letter **away**.*
- They are never used in the mid position, but you can sometimes put them in the initial position. For example: ***Out** they went. **Up** we climbed.*
- Adverbs that are part of a phrasal verb can come between the verb and its object. For example, you can say, "*She switched the TV **off**,*" or "*She switched **off** the TV.*" However, if the object is a pronoun, the adverb must come after it.
- **Adverbs of degree** usually come before the word they describe. For example: *I am **rather** proud of this picture. They worked **very** hard. No-one **strongly** disagreed.* If this word is a verb, the adverb can also come in the end position. For example: No-one disagreed **strongly**.

D ***Ten of the adverbs in this passage are in the wrong positions. Circle each mistake and rewrite the passage correctly on the lines below.***

If the fire alarm rings, you must leave immediately the building. Walk to the assembly point calmly by the main gate and there wait until a member of staff tells you what to do. Do not panic and run, because you might fall over and hurt yourself.

People ignore sometimes a fire alarm, thinking that it is just being tested, or that it accidentally has been set off. This extremely is foolish. You should assume that always there is a real fire, even if you cannot see any flames or smell any smoke.

Some people have valuable possessions and do not want to behind leave

 ISBN 978-81-8477-752-9

them. They often waste time picking up these things instead of straight going to the exit. Remember that your life is your most valuable possession. Do not throw away it!

Grammar Help

The adverb **only** should be placed as close as possible to the word it refers to. Moving it around can change the meaning of the sentence. For example:

__Only__ Jane heard the helicopter. (= No-one else heard it.)
Jane __only__ heard the helicopter. (= She did not see it.)
Jane heard __only__ the helicopter. (= She did not hear anything else.)

E ***Rewrite these sentences with only in the required position to give the meaning in brackets.***

1. Tom has two sisters.

_______________________________ (= He does not have three sisters.)

 ISBN 978-81-8477-752-9

2. The factory makes cars.

_______________________________________ (= It does not make anything else.)

3. This bus goes to the station.

_______________________________________ (= No other buses go there.)

4. My finger hurts when I bend it.

_______________________________________ (= It does not hurt at other times.)

5. Mum washed the dishes.

_______________________________________ (= She did not dry them.)

 ISBN 978-81-8477-752-9

14 Prepositions

Grammar Help

Prepositions link words and phrases to a following noun or pronoun, with a variety of meanings.

- Prepositions of position include **in, on, at** and **under.** For example: *They live* ***in*** *an apartment. I found my slippers* ***under*** *the bed.*
- Prepositions of direction are chiefly used with verbs of movement. They include **up, down, across** and **towards**. For example: *The squirrel ran* ***up*** *a tree. We skated* ***across*** *the ice.*
- Prepositions of time include **before, after, until** and **during**. For example: *You should wash your hands* ***before*** *meals. It rained* ***during*** *the night.*
- Do not confuse the prepositions of time **since** and **for**. The preposition **since** comes after a verb in a perfect tense and before a date or an event. For example: *They have been very busy* ***since*** *the birth of their baby.* The preposition **for,** which can come after a verb in any tense, comes before a period of time. For example: *They sailed south* ***for*** *two days.*

A ***Underline the prepositions in the following sentences. Are they prepositions of position (P) or direction (D)? Write the correct letter in the box.***

1. The milk is in the fridge. ☐
2. The horse jumped over the fence. ☐
3. She wore a gold necklace around her neck. ☐
4. Tom fell down the stairs. ☐
5. Mum will drive us to the station. ☐
6. There is a bookstore at the airport. ☐
7. A car drove through the puddle and splashed us. ☐

 ISBN 978-81-8477-752-9

8. The spilt coffee left a brown stain on the carpet. [ ]

9. Dad framed the picture and hung it above the fireplace. [ ]

10. The train from Lahore has just arrived. [ ]

B ***Fill in the blanks with since, for or until.***

1. Mr Jones has taught at this school ____________ 2005.
2. The baby has been crying ____________ nearly an hour.
3. He has been living alone ____________ the death of his wife.
4. She lay in bed ____________ 10 o'clock.
5. They stayed with us ____________ a week.
6. No-one may leave ____________ the end of the meeting.
7. Grandma has felt much better ____________ her operation.
8. Wait ____________ a few minutes, then try again.
9. I have not seen Mary ____________ last Monday.
10. The new building will not be finished ____________ next April.

C ***Write ten sentences of your own using a verb from box A, a preposition from box B and a noun from box C.***

A | cycle | eat | feel | fly | hide | lie | snow | swim | wait | work

B | across | at | down | in | behind | on | during | before | outside | over

C | city | day | door | exam | ground | hill | river | supermarket | theatre | winter

____

____

____

 ISBN 978-81-8477-752-9

Grammar Help

- Many prepositions can have different uses in different contexts. For example, **at** can be a preposition of time or position (as in **at** *midnight* and **at** *the supermarket*), **from** can be a preposition of time or direction (as in **from** *Tuesday onwards* and *the flight* **from** *London*) and **under** can be a preposition of position or direction (as in "*Your slippers are* **under** *the bed*" and "*The boat sailed* **under** *the bridge*").
- There are many other prepositions with a variety of meanings. For example, **of** can mean "containing" (as in *a box* **of** *chocolates*) or "belonging to" (as in *the roof* **of** *the house*). The preposition **with** can mean "using" (as in *I cut it* **with** *a knife*) or "accompanying" (as in *I went* **with** *my friend*).

D ***Write pairs of sentences using the given preposition in two different ways. The first one has been done as an example.***

1. **(on)** Your keys are on the table.
   (on) I have a dentist's appointment on Friday.
2. **(by)** ______
   (by) ______
3. **(for)** ______
   (for) ______
4. **(to)** ______
   (to) ______

 ISBN 978-81-8477-752-9

5. **(past)** ______________________

(past) ______________________

6. **(in)** ______________________

(in) ______________________

7. **(after)** ______________________

(after) ______________________

8. **(without)** ______________________

(without) ______________________

9. **(over)** ______________________

(over) ______________________

10. **(across)** ______________________

(across) ______________________

E ***Fill in the blanks with the prepositions from the box. Use each word only once.***

aboard	about	in	after	off	around	at	during	by	for
from	across	of	along	on	through	to	until	up	with

Peter Smith is sailing ______________ the world ______________ his yacht. He originally planned to do this single-handed: that is, ______________ himself. However, he realized that it would be easier, safer and probably more fun to make the long journey ______________ another person ______________ the boat. Several of his friends volunteered to help him, and he chose the one who knew the most ______________ sailing.

 ISBN 978-81-8477-752-9

The yacht was moored at Southampton, ________________ the south coast of England. Peter and his friend sailed it ________________ the English Channel ________________ France, then made their way ________________ the coast to Spain. They had to wait there ________________ several days, because the weather was not suitable for crossing the Atlantic Ocean. Peter did not mind the delay. It gave him an opportunity to fix some minor problems that had occurred on the boat ________________ the first part of their journey. These included climbing ________________ the mast to change a light bulb ________________ the top.

They finally set off ________________ Spain and arrived at the Caribbean island of Barbados three weeks later. When they first stepped ________________ the boat onto dry land their legs felt rather shaky ________________ so many days at sea. They spent a very pleasant month exploring the Caribbean, then made their way ________________ the Panama Canal to the Pacific Ocean. Peter was heading for New Zealand, but he did not want to arrive there ________________ November, which is late spring in that country. This gave them plenty of time to visit some of the islands of the Pacific Ocean on the way. They finally arrived in New Zealand a few days ago, and are currently planning the next part ________________ their voyage.

 ISBN 978-81-8477-752-9

Grammar Help

- Some **prepositions** can also be adverbs or conjunctions, or both. For example:

  *I read a book **before** lunch.* (preposition)
  *I have read this book **before**.* (adverb)
  *I read a book **before** I went to bed.* (conjunction)
- The word is an **adverb** if it does not link a verb to a following noun or pronoun.
- The word is a **conjunction** if it is followed by a clause (part of a sentence containing a verb).

F ***Are the words in bold print prepositions (P), adverbs (A) or conjunctions (C)? Write the correct letter in the box.***

1. The bird perched **on** the fence. ☐
2. Jane took her coat **off** and went into the lounge. ☐
3. They ran **up** the hill to the bus stop. ☐
4. I have not seen Tom **since** he went to university. ☐
5. The teacher told the students to put **down** their pens. ☐
6. My sister is taller **than** I am. ☐

 ISBN 978-81-8477-752-9

15 Transitional Devices

Grammar Help

Transitional devices, also called connectors, link sentences or parts of sentences together.

- The simplest types of transitional devices are the conjunctions **and**, **but** and **or**. They can link single words, phrases or clauses (parts of a sentence containing a verb). For example: *The water was cool* ***and*** *refreshing. I shouted for help* ***but*** *no-one heard me. You can read a book* ***or*** *play a computer game.*
- Words like **because**, **when**, **if** and **although** are also conjunctions. They usually link clauses within a sentence. For example: *She went to bed* ***because*** *she felt tired. Ask the teacher* ***if*** *you do not understand.*
- Other types of transitional devices are linking adverbs such as **however**, **then**, **firstly** and **therefore**. They often come at the beginning of a sentence, connecting it to the one before. For example: *It was a fine, sunny day.* ***However***, *the wind was rather cold.*
- Some transitional devices consist of more than one word, such as **so that**, **for example** and **on the contrary**. For example: *This puzzle is not easy.* ***On the contrary***, *it is one of the most difficult puzzles I have ever tried to solve.*

A ***Choose the correct word from the brackets to fill in each blank.***

1. Kate was lonely ________________ (because/if) she had no friends.
2. Do you live in a house ________________ (but/or) an apartment?
3. I read a book ________________ (when/while) I waited for the train.
4. He wore a raincoat ________________ (although/since) it was not raining.
5. France is in Europe ________________ (and/as) China is in Asia.
6. Put up your hand ________________ (after/if) you know the answer.
7. You should brush your teeth ________________ (before/while) you go to bed.
8. A spider has eight legs. ________________ (However/Therefore) it is not an insect.
9. I helped the old man ________________ (because/but) he did not thank me.
10. The show will not begin ________________ (until/when) everyone stops talking.

 ISBN 978-81-8477-752-9

B ***Complete the sentences with one of the phrases or clauses from the box.***

her grandfather died	**I did not have enough money**
I'll make a pot of tea	**Sally got out of bed**
tell the police	**the car would not start**
we were late	**they can cause tooth decay**
Tom rang his friend's house	**you leave the building**

1. The battery was flat. As a result, ______________________________.
2. If you notice anything suspicious, ______________________________.
3. ______________________________ when our guests arrive.
4. The teacher was angry because ______________________________.
5. ______________________________ as soon as her alarm clock went off.
6. Before ______________________________, check that all the windows are shut.
7. She has been unhappy since ______________________________.
8. ______________________________. However, Dad offered to lend me some.
9. There are several reasons why sweets are bad for you. Firstly, ______________________________
______________________________.
10. ______________________________ but no one answered the phone.

 ISBN 978-81-8477-752-9

Grammar Help

Transitional devices can serve various purposes.

- Connectors such as **and, also, as well as, in addition** and **furthermore** show addition. For example: *Tom broke his ankle when he fell down the steps. He* ***also*** *bruised his knees.*
- Connectors such as **or, alternatively** and **instead** introduce an alternative. For example: *Do not drive to the city centre. Go there by bus* ***instead****.*
- The connectors **as** and **than** are used in comparisons. For example: *James can run faster* ***than*** *I can.*
- Connectors such as **but, although, however, whereas** and **on the other hand** express contrast. For example: *African elephants have large ears* ***whereas*** *Indian elephants have small ears.*
- Connectors such as **for example, such as, namely** and **that is** introduce an illustration or more specific information. For example: *Lions and tigers are carnivores.* ***That is,*** *they eat meat.*
- The connectors **if, unless** and **provided that** introduce a condition. For example: *I shall not go* ***unless*** *it stops raining.*
- Connectors such as **first** (or **firstly**), **second** (or **secondly**), **then, next** and **finally** introduce the items of a sequence. For example: ***First*** *switch the computer on,* ***then*** *type your password in the box.*
- Connectors such as **before, after, when, until, while** and **as** show how actions or events are related in time. For example: *Remember to brush your teeth* ***before*** *you go to bed.*
- Connectors such as **to sum up, in conclusion** and **all in all** introduce a conclusion. For example: ***All in all,*** *the festival was a great success.*
- The connectors **because, as** and **since** introduce a cause or a reason. For example: *Billy went home early* ***because*** *he did not feel well.*
- Connectors such as **therefore, consequently, so** and **as a result** introduce an effect or a result. For example: *Jane did not work very hard.* ***As a result,*** *she failed her exams.*

C ***Each sentence contains an incorrect transitional device. Replace it with the correct one and rewrite the sentence on the line below.***

1. The journey did not take as long than we thought it might.

____

2. There was no lemonade left, because I had a drink of water instead.

____

 ISBN 978-81-8477-752-9

3. They did not stop running while they reached the end of the road.

____

4. She cannot speak English, whereas she has lived in England for five years.

____

5. Tom entered the competition and he did not win a prize.

____

6. I finished my homework, after I went to bed.

____

D ***Write a sentence (or a pair of linked sentences) of your own in which a transitional device is used for the purpose given in brackets. The first one has been done to help you.***

1. (addition) The game is too difficult for young children. Furthermore, it could be dangerous.
2. (time) ____
3. (conclusion) ____
4. (comparison) ____
5. (illustration) ____
6. (condition) ____
7. (alternative) ____
8. (sequence) ____

 ISBN 978-81-8477-752-9

9. (contrast) ____

____

10. (effect) ____

____

11. (cause) ____

____

12. (addition) ____

____

E ***Fill in each blank with an appropriate transitional device.***

When you have to write an essay, how do you set about the task? There are several things to attend to ____________ you start writing the actual text.

____________ you should draft an outline. Remember that an essay must have a beginning, a middle and an end. Make some notes about the subject, ____________ do not try to compose whole paragraphs at this stage. ____________ you might find it useful to write the topic sentence for each paragraph ____________ you draw up your plan.

____________ you should think about the people who will read the essay. Do they know a lot ____________ a little about the subject? ____________ they are they likely to be unfamiliar with it, you will need to explain things clearly. You will ____________ need to use simple language that is easy to understand.

____________ you can write the essay itself. Remember that the text should be interesting to read, ____________ being factually correct. ____________ you have finished, read the essay through ____________ correct any mistakes you have made. Do not hand it in ____________ you are sure that it is as good as it can be.

 ISBN 978-81-8477-752-9

16 Punctuation and Capitalization

Grammar Help

- You put a **full stop**, **question mark** or **exclamation mark** at the end of a sentence. For example: *It is raining. How old are you? Come here at once!*
- You use an **apostrophe** to show possession (usually followed by **s**), or where letters have been removed in a contraction. For example: *This is Jane's book. I've lost my key.*
- You use a **comma** to separate items in lists. For example: *She was wearing a coat, a hat, a scarf, gloves and boots.* (You do not need a comma before **and**.)
- You also put a **comma** before the opening or closing quotation mark in direct speech, to separate it from the saying verb. For example: *Jane asked, "What is that bird?" "It is an eagle," her father replied.*
- You use a **colon** to introduce a list. For example: *Four people live in this house: my mother, my father, my sister and me.* However, you do not add a colon if the list is the object of a verb or preposition. For example: *The shop sells books, cards, pens and paper.*
- You also use a **colon** to introduce a long quotation, or after the name of each speaker in a play. For example: *The British statesman Winston Churchill said: "We shall fight on the beaches, we shall fight on the landing grounds, we shall fight in the fields and in the streets, we shall fight in the hills; we shall never surrender."*

A ***Add the missing punctuation to the following dialogue.***

Tom Where are you going

Sue Im off to the supermarket Mum has asked me to buy some food for Dads birthday party tomorrow She wants bread cheese eggs tomatoes cakes and biscuits

Tom How many people are coming to the party

Sue Im not sure I think Mum has invited about fifteen people Grandma

 ISBN 978-81-8477-752-9

Grandpa Aunt Mary Uncle Bill our four cousins and some of Dads friends

Tom Does Dad know about the party yet

Sue No Its still a surprise I hope hell be pleased

Tom Hush Here he comes Lets talk about something else

B ***Complete these sentences with a list of four items, adding the correct punctuation. The first one has been done to help you.***

1. You need the following ingredients: flour, sugar, eggs and butter.
2. Mary has four pets ____________________
3. I went to the greengrocer's and bought ____________________
4. The kit contains the following tools ____________________
5. These boys have been chosen for the team ____________________
6. A stationer's shop sells ____________________
7. The airline flies to the following countries ____________________
8. Joe is very musical. He can play ____________________
9. What would you like to drink ____________________
10. Mum made new curtains for ____________________
11. You can travel to the airport by ____________________
12. There are four shops in the village ____________________

 ISBN 978-81-8477-752-9

Grammar Help

- A proper noun begins with a capital letter. Proper nouns are the names of places, people, days, months, festivals, languages, religions, etc. For example: ***P**akistan, **M**ichael, **T**uesday, **A**ugust, **C**hristmas, **E**nglish, **B**uddhism.*
- Some other words that are part of the name also have capital initials. For example: ***M**r Brown, **A**unt Sally, **M**ount Fuji, **L**ake Victoria, Station **R**oad.* However, words like **the** and **of** do not have capital initials. For example: ***t**he Pacific Ocean, **t**he United States **o**f America.*
- When you write the title of a book or film, you put a capital letter at the beginning of the first word and all other words that are not articles, prepositions or conjunctions. For example: *The **G**irl with a **P**earl **E**arring, **A** **H**istory of the **U**niverse.*

C1. ***Can you find 20 proper nouns in the word puzzle? The words may be written across or down. Draw a line through each one you find.***

M	A	C	C	A	N	D	R	Y	F	L	P
F	X	H	U	P	A	C	I	F	I	C	Z
R	O	I	M	J	L	A	P	R	I	L	M
I	E	N	G	L	I	S	H	A	B	M	A
D	D	A	X	E	C	M	O	N	D	A	Y
A	E	W	A	V	E	N	R	C	U	L	R
Y	C	O	G	E	Z	V	Q	E	P	A	A
P	E	T	E	R	D	I	J	U	L	Y	M
R	M	I	L	E	T	H	A	M	E	S	A
K	B	A	I	S	L	A	M	P	W	V	D
D	E	A	F	T	U	S	E	B	X	R	A
U	R	D	U	G	L	A	S	I	A	P	N

 ISBN 978-81-8477-752-9

C2. ***Now use ten of the words in sentences of your own that state a fact about the noun. Try to choose words of different types, such as a place, a language, a person's name, a day, a month, and so on.***

D ***Here are some titles of famous books with the words in the wrong order and no capital letters. Rewrite each title correctly on the line below.***

1. of rings the lord the

2. wind the in willows the

3. potter the fire and harry of goblet

4. in adventures wonderland alice's

5. two of tale a cities

6. chocolate the factory and charlie

 ISBN 978-81-8477-752-9

7. one hundred and the dalmatians

8. tom of the sawyer adventures

9. other family and my animals

10. beaker of the tracy story

E ***Each sentence contains at least one error of punctuation or capitalization (sometimes more than one). Rewrite them correctly.***

1. Aunt Mary and uncle Jack have three children: Paul Kate and Lily.

2. "I have'nt told anyone your secret." said Joe.

3. Do you know where they live.

4. I watched a television programme called "One Man and his Dog" at my friends house.

5. Paul replied: "We're nearly there".

6. "James And The Giant Peach" is a childrens' book.

7. The bird's are building a nest.

8. I asked her where she was going?

9. The man was carrying: a briefcase and an umbrella.

 ISBN 978-81-8477-752-9

10. The bank, is at the end of North street.

11. May I borrow your pen!

12. We stayed, at The Hilton Hotel.

 ISBN 978-81-8477-752-9

17 Affirmative and Negative Sentences

Grammar Help

A declarative sentence can be affirmative or negative.

- A **negative** sentence contains one of the following words: **not**, **never**, **no**, **none**, **no one**, **nothing**, **nowhere**, **neither**, **nor**. For example: *It is* ***not*** *raining. I have* ***never*** *been to England.* ***No one*** *laughed.*
- An **affirmative** sentence (also called a **positive** sentence) does not contain any negative words. Sometimes it has a different word in place of the negative one. For example: *It is raining. I have been to England. There are* ***some*** *spoons in the drawer.* ***Everyone*** *laughed.*
- Remember that you should not use two negative words in the same clause. The only exception to this rule is **neither** and **nor**, which are often used together. For example: ***Neither*** *Tom* ***nor*** *Bill had enough money to pay the bill.*

A ***Are these sentences affirmative (A) or negative (N)? Write the correct letter in the box.***

1. Neither of the shops was open. ☐
2. Our teacher gave us some useful advice. ☐
3. There was nowhere to hide. ☐
4. I will never make the same mistake again. ☐
5. The box contained a valuable diamond necklace. ☐
6. This is not a good idea. ☐
7. He refused to lend me any money. ☐
8. Alice has had nothing to eat all day. ☐
9. David told no one about his secret fear. ☐
10. You should be nicer to your little sister. ☐

 ISBN 978-81-8477-752-9

B ***Fill in the blanks in this short narrative with the negative words from the box, using a different one each time.***

neither	never	no	none	no one	not	nothing	nowhere

Jane was struggling with her maths homework. She did ____________ understand one of the questions. She asked her parents, but ____________ of them had time to help her. They were both too busy. There was ____________ else in the house that Jane could turn to. Her brother was in his bedroom, playing a computer game, but it was ____________ use asking him. He was younger than Jane, and he had ____________ been any good at maths. Jane's elder sister might have been able to help, but she was ____________ to be found. "She is probably out with her boyfriend," thought Jane. "I am going to have to solve this problem on my own. I'm sure I can do it if I try. ____________ is impossible!"

Jane read the question again, and thought about it very hard. Eventually she worked out the answer, and felt very proud of herself. She felt even more proud when her teacher marked the homework. ____________ of the other students had solved the problem, so Jane was the only one who got full marks.

 ISBN 978-81-8477-752-9

Now use each of these words in a negative sentence of your own.

____

____

____

____

____

____

____

____

Grammar Help

- You make the verb **be** negative by adding **not** after it. For example: *This **is** my jacket.* → *This **is not** my jacket. They **were** afraid of the dog.* → *They **were not** afraid of the dog.*
- You use **does/do/did not** to make other verbs in the simple present or simple past negative. For example: *She **likes** chocolate.* → *She **does not like** chocolate. The bomb **exploded**.* → *The bomb **did not explode**.* (Remember that you use the base form of the verb after the helping verb **do**.)
- There are different rules for the negative word **never**. You put it after **be** and before other verbs in the simple present or simple past. For example: *Jack **is never** late for school. Our dog **never barks**. My grandmother **never learnt** to speak English.*
- If the verb consists of a helping or modal verb followed by a participle or base form, you add **not** or **never** after the first part of the verb. For example: *It **is not** raining. You **should not** be so careless. The car **has not** been repaired. I **have never** read that book. We will **never** see her again.* (Remember that the negative form of **can** is **cannot**.)
- Remember that **some** can change to **no** or **not ... any** in a negative sentence. For example: *There is **some** milk in the fridge.* → *There is **no** milk in the fridge. She lent me **some** money.* → *She did **not** lend me **any** money.*

 ISBN 978-81-8477-752-9

C Change these affirmative sentences to negative sentences.

1. Jane is Paul's sister.

____

2. The men worked very hard.

____

3. Everyone clapped at the end of the show.

____

4. The newsagent sells English newspapers.

____

5. I can run as fast as you.

____

6. All of my friends like this kind of music.

____

7. Alice was wearing her best clothes.

____

8. There is something wrong with this computer.

____

9. The animals have been fed.

____

10. Joe is sometimes rude to his parents.

____

D Change these negative sentences to affirmative sentences.

1. Mum was not in the kitchen.

____

2. The soup did not smell very nice.

____

 ISBN 978-81-8477-752-9

3. They have done nothing about the problem.

4. The patient is not feeling better.

5. Mary does not know what to do.

6. The dog will not bite you.

7. James never cycles to school.

8. These boots do not fit me.

9. There are no spelling mistakes in this book.

10. The woman had nowhere else to go.

E ***Each of these negative sentences contains an error. Rewrite them correctly on the lines below.***

1. The children were listening not to their teacher.

2. We did not see no monkeys at the zoo.

3. These dishes have been not washed properly.

4. I never have travelled in a helicopter.

5. Mary invited not Sam to her party.

 ISBN 978-81-8477-752-9

6. They never do nothing to help.

____

7. The meat must be not eaten raw.

____

8. I could not find my mobile phone nowhere.

____

9. There is not need to worry.

____

10. It does matter not where you sit.

____

Grammar Help

In informal speech and writing, the word **not** can be shortened to **n't**, forming the contractions **isn't, aren't, wasn't, weren't, doesn't, don't, haven't, won't** (for **will not**), **shouldn't, can't** (for **cannot**), **mustn't**, etc. For example: *I **don't** like cabbage. The door **won't** shut.*

F ***Fill in each blank in this dialogue with a different negative contraction.***

Kate: I ______________ find my jacket.

Paul: There's one on the chair over there.

Kate: I know, but it ______________ mine. My jacket ______________ have a zip up the front. It has buttons instead. Mum will go mad if I've lost it. I ______________ had it very long, and it was quite expensive. I hope someone else ______________ taken it by mistake.

Paul: Why ______________ you go to the lost property office?

 ISBN 978-81-8477-752-9

Kate: I've already been, but there ____________ anyone there.

Paul: I'd like to help you look for it, but I have to go. I have a piano lesson, and I ____________ be late.

Kate: I ____________ know you were learning the piano. Are you any good at it?

Paul: Not really, but my teacher said I ____________ give up trying. He said anyone can learn to play well if they do enough practice.

Now use five more negative contractions in sentences of your own.

____

____

____

____

____

 ISBN 978-81-8477-752-9

18 Imperative Sentences

Grammar Help

- Imperative sentences are used to give commands or instructions. For example: ***Stop*** *talking.* ***Press*** *the green button.*
- The imperative form of a verb is the base form, such as **be, do, come** or **put**. You use it without a subject, usually at the beginning of the sentence or clause. For example: ***Be*** *quiet.* ***Remove*** *the empty ink cartridge and* ***replace*** *it with the new one.*
- Imperative sentences usually end with a full stop, but some commands spoken urgently or angrily end with an exclamation mark. For example: *Get out of my way! Come here at once!*
- You can make a command sound more polite by putting **please** at the beginning or end. For example: *Stop talking,* ***please. Please*** *pass me the water jug.*

A ***Fill in the blanks with the imperative verbs from the box.***

be	**close**	**give**	**lock**	**mix**	**peel**	**read**	**show**	**throw**	**turn**	**wipe**	**write**

1. ____________________ your feet on the mat.
2. ____________________ the flour and water together.
3. ____________________ your name at the top of the paper.
4. Please ____________________ me what to do.
5. ____________________ this note to your mother.
6. ____________________ the instructions carefully.
7. ____________________ the handle to the right.
8. Please ____________________ more careful in future.
9. ____________________ the door and ____________________ it.
10. ____________________ the banana and ____________________ the skin away.

 ISBN 978-81-8477-752-9

B ***Underline all the imperative verbs in these recipe instructions.***

Put the sugar and butter in a bowl and whisk them together until the mixture is thick and creamy. You will get the best results if you use an electric mixer or food processor. Then add the beaten eggs and flour and mix thoroughly. Pour the mixture into a baking pan and cook it in a preheated oven for twenty minutes. When the cake is ready, it should be slightly brown on the top and firm to the touch.

Remove the cake from the baking pan and leave it to cool. Meanwhile, prepare the filling by chopping up the strawberries and mixing them with the whipped cream. Finally, cut the cake in two across the middle, spread the strawberries and cream on one half and then put the other half on top. If you do not intend to serve or eat the cake straight away, you must store it in a cool place.

Grammar Help

- A negative imperative sentence usually has **do not** or **don't** before the main verb. For example: *Please* ***do not*** *walk on the grass.* ***Don't*** *be so rude!*
- You can also use **never** to make the sentence negative. For example: ***Never*** *stop trying!*

C ***Write an imperative sentence that will produce the given result. The first one has been done as an example.***

1. Draw a picture of your house.
   The children drew pictures of their houses.
2. ______________________________
   I took the bottles to the recycling bin.

 ISBN 978-81-8477-752-9

3. Don't ____________________
The boy was not frightened.

4. ____________________
She helped herself to another piece of cake.

5. Please ____________________
We made less noise.

6. ____________________
They did as they were told.

7. ____________________
He wore smart clothes for his interview.

8. Do not ____________________
I ate fewer sweets.

9. ____________________
I wrote my phone number on the piece of paper she gave me.

10. Do not ____________________
We got off our bikes and pushed them along the footpath.

11. Please ____________________
Nobody touched the exhibits.

12. ____________________
I knew the answer, so I put up my hand.

13. ____________________
We turned left at the crossroads and saw the hotel on our right.

14. Never ____________________
I have told no-one my secret password.

15. ____________________
I could not guess where she was going the following day.

D ***Fill in the blanks with appropriate verbs.***

We can all do something to help protect the environment and the natural world by following these simple rules:

1. Do not ____________ short distances by car. ____________ or ____________ by bike instead.

 ISBN 978-81-8477-752-9

2. For longer journeys, ________________ use of public transport if it is available.
3. ________________ electricity whenever and wherever you can. ________________ off lights in empty rooms and do not ________________ the TV on when no one is watching it.
4. ________________ alternative sources of energy, such as wind power or solar power, if possible.
5. Do not ________________ water. ________________ a shower instead of having a bath.
6. ________________ as much of your rubbish as you can.
7. Do not ________________ litter on the ground.
8. Do not ________________ anything that might harm the wildlife of an area.
9. ________________ things that are locally produced if possible, rather than things that have been imported from other countries.
10. ________________ your friends and family to follow these rules too.

E ***What might you say in the following situations? Write an imperative sentence for each. The first one has been done as an example.***

1. Your brother has snatched the book you were reading.
   Give me back my book!
2. You cannot do your homework on your own.
   ____
3. Someone is about to put their hand on a door you have just painted.
   ____
4. There is a draught from an open window.
   ____
5. You are reminding your friend to send you a postcard.
   ____
6. Some visitors have just arrived, tired from their journey.
   ____
7. Your sister is disturbing you when you are busy.
   ____

 ISBN 978-81-8477-752-9

8. Someone has not noticed that they are in danger.

____

9. The music coming from your neighbour's radio is too loud.

____

10. Your parents are going to a party.

____

11. Someone is feeling anxious.

____

12. You want to borrow your friend's calculator.

____

F ***Complete the following sentences with a suitable imperative clause. The first one has been done as an example.***

1. When the kettle boils, make the tea.
2. If you have toothache, _______________.
3. When you have finished your meal, _______________.
4. If it starts raining, _______________.
5. Before you leave the room, _______________.
6. If the milk has gone sour, _______________.
7. When the letter arrives, _______________.
8. If you are too hot, _______________.
9. Before you hand in your essay, _______________.
10. If the phone rings, _______________.
11. After you have washed the towels, _______________.
12. If you don't know how to spell the word, _______________.
13. Before you wrap the gift, _______________.
14. If someone is bullying you at school, _______________.
15. If the dog scratches at the door, _______________.

 ISBN 978-81-8477-752-9

19 Conditional Sentences

Grammar Help

- A conditional sentence usually contains a clause beginning with **if** or **unless**. For example: ***If*** *everyone helps, the job will soon be finished. Do not phone this number* ***unless*** *there is an emergency.*
- The two examples above are **first conditional** sentences. The verb in the **if/unless**-clause is in the present tense. The verb in the other clause (the main clause) is in the future tense or in the imperative. An **if**-clause can come before or after the main clause, but an **unless**-clause usually comes second.
- First conditional sentences express a real possibility. They talk about something that is likely to happen.
- Sometimes **can** is used in either clause of a first conditional sentence. For example: *He* ***cannot*** *fix the clock if he does not have the right tools. Do not go in the water unless you* ***can*** *swim.*

A ***Fill in the blanks with the correct forms of the given verbs, in the right order.***

1. They cannot ____________ us if we do not ____________ them our address. (give, visit)
2. If he ____________ this race, he will ____________ the world champion. (become, win)
3. She will not ____________ you unless you ____________ loudly. (hear, speak)
4. If you ____________ the hotplate, you will ____________ yourself. (burn, touch)
5. I will ____________ you if the patient's condition ____________. (improve, tell)
6. If the expressway ____________ busy, we will ____________ a different route. (be, take)
7. We will not ____________ her unless she ____________ a good job. (do, pay)
8. You will ____________ the baby if you ____________ a lot of noise. (make, wake)

 ISBN 978-81-8477-752-9

9. If James does not ____________________ soon, he will ____________________ the train. (arrive, miss)

10. You will not ____________________ your bag back unless the police ____________________ the thief. (catch, get)

B ***Match the clauses in box A with those in box B to create ten first conditional sentences.***

A	B
If you have flu,	change the battery.
You will be late for school	unless all your answers are correct.
Do not make a statement	if I cannot access the internet.
You will not get full marks	keep your germs to yourself.
If the torch stops working,	if you don't leave soon.
You can come with us	take it to the police station.
If you find the stolen necklace,	if you are thirsty.
I will not be able to read my emails	unless you are good at science.
You cannot become a doctor	if you want to.
Help yourself to a drink	unless you are sure it is true.

____

____

____

____

____

____

____

____

____

____

 ISBN 978-81-8477-752-9

Grammar Help

- A second conditional sentence usually contains an **if**-clause. (Clauses beginning with **unless** are uncommon in second conditional sentences.) The modal verb **would** is used in the main clause. The verb in the **if**-clause is in the simple past tense. For example: *If everyone **helped**, the job **would** soon be finished. She **would** get better marks if she **worked** harder.*
- Second conditional sentences express a hypothetical possibility. That is, they talk about something that could happen but probably will not.
- Sometimes the main clause of a second conditional sentence contains **could** instead of **would**. For example: *He **could** fix the clock if he had the right tools.*
- You often use **were** instead of **was** in the **if**-clause of a second conditional sentence, especially if it refers to something that is impossible. For example: *If I **were** a boy, I could join the football team.*

C ***Are these first conditional sentences (1) or second conditional sentences (2)? Write the correct number in the box.***

1. I could see more clearly if the light were brighter. ☐
2. If you get lost, look at the map. ☐
3. She will never walk again unless she has this operation. ☐
4. If Jane were here, she would know what to do. ☐
5. You could grow your own vegetables if you had a larger garden. ☐
6. If we had a telescope, we could look at the stars. ☐
7. If you like chocolate, you will love this cake. ☐
8. The car would go faster if there weren't so many people in it. ☐
9. Throw the can in the bin if it is not recyclable. ☐
10. You cannot go on the school trip unless you have your parents' permission. ☐

 ISBN 978-81-8477-752-9

D Fill in the blanks with *will* or *would*.

1. He ____________________ get into trouble if the teacher catches him doing that.
2. If you were fitter, you ____________________ be able to walk further.
3. My brother ____________________ lie in bed all morning if he did not have to go to work.
4. I ____________________ not forgive her unless she apologizes.
5. If they were older and wiser, they ____________________ not take such foolish risks.
6. I ____________________ wash my hair if I had any shampoo.
7. They ____________________ not be allowed in unless they have tickets.
8. I ____________________ not eat nuts if I were allergic to them.
9. If you do not pay attention, you ____________________ not understand.
10. The match ____________________ be cancelled if it rains.

E1. Rewrite these first conditional sentences as second conditional sentences.

1. I will have to walk home if I miss the bus.

   ____

2. If the volcano erupts, the village will be destroyed.

   ____

3. You will feel cooler if you roll up your sleeves.

   ____

4. If no one waters the plants, they will die.

   ____

5. My parents will be angry with me if I fail my exams.

   ____

E2. Rewrite these second conditional sentences as first conditional sentences.

1. If you refused her offer she would be offended.

   ____

 ISBN 978-81-8477-752-9

2. The dog would run away if I left the gate open.

____

3. If I won first prize, I would feel very proud.

____

4. He would go if he could afford the fare.

____

5. If she found out the truth, she would be very upset.

____

F ***Fill in the blanks with the correct form of the given verb.***

1. Be quiet unless you ______________ something interesting to say. (have)
2. If more people ______________, the service would improve. (complain)
3. She would like you better if you ______________ nicer to her. (be)
4. If Mum ______________ out, she will be angry. (find)
5. The room would look better if you ______________ the walls a different colour. (paint)
6. I will phone you if my flight ______________ delayed. (be)
7. If he ______________ his hair cut, he would look much smarter. (have)
8. If you ______________ your watch, you would not know what time it was. (lose)
9. Rock the baby's cradle if it ______________ crying. (start)
10. If you ______________ this opportunity, you will regret it for the rest of your life. (waste)

G ***Complete these sentences with a suitable main clause.***

1. If I were good at art, ______________________________.
2. If I had a boat, ______________________________.
3. If I were a millionaire, ______________________________.
4. If I lived in a bigger house, ______________________________.
5. If I were president, ______________________________.

 ISBN 978-81-8477-752-9

20 Active and Passive Voice

Grammar Help

- When a verb is in the **active voice,** the subject is the person or thing that does the action. For example: *The chef* ***cooks*** *the meals. Jane* ***helped*** *me. The birds* ***were singing****. The wind* ***has blown*** *the fence down.*
- When a verb is in the **passive voice,** the subject is the person or thing that receives the action. A passive verb consists of a helping verb **be** followed by a past participle. For example: *The meals* ***are cooked*** *by the chef. I* ***was helped*** *by Jane. The fence* ***has been blown*** *down.*

A ***Are the verbs in these sentences in the active voice (A) or the passive voice (P)? Write the correct letter in the box.***

1. Elephants are found in Africa and Asia. ☐
2. The sun rises in the east. ☐
3. Jane was being bullied at school. ☐
4. The disease can be treated with antibiotics. ☐
5. Our teacher told us the correct answer. ☐
6. The dog is chasing the cat. ☐
7. The house has not yet been sold. ☐
8. Tom will help you with your homework. ☐
9. We have lived here for ten years. ☐
10. These photos were taken by my grandmother. ☐

B ***Fill in the blanks in these passive sentences with the correct form of the given verb.***

1. Sally has been ____________________ a prize. (give)

 ISBN 978-81-8477-752-9

2. Little is ____________________ about the people who lived here. (know)
3. Flowers were ____________________ on the soldiers' graves. (lay)
4. You will be ____________________ how to program a computer. (teach)
5. The climbers are being ____________________ to safety by the rescue team. (lead)
6. All the seams are ____________________ by hand. (sew)
7. We have not been ____________________ what to do. (tell)
8. Too much food is being needlessly ____________________ away. (throw)
9. The butter should be ____________________ more thinly. (spread)
10. I was ____________________ by a loud noise. (wake)

Grammar Help

- When you change a sentence from active to passive, the **object** of the active verb becomes the **subject** of the passive verb. For example: My *grandfather owns* ***all these houses.*** → ***All these houses*** *are owned by my grandfather.* (Notice that the verb changes from singular to plural to match the new subject.)
- The subject of the active verb is sometimes given at the end of the passive sentence, usually after the preposition **by**, as in the example above. However, this is not necessary if the "doer" of the action is obvious or unimportant. For example, you can change "*The wind has blown the fence down*" to "*The fence has been blown down,* without adding *by the wind,*" because nothing else is likely to have performed the action.
- The tense of the helping verb **be** in the passive voice is the same as the tense of the active verb. In other words, you use **am/is/are** + past participle for the present tense and **was/were** + past participle for the past tense. For example: *takes* → *am/is/are taken; broke* → *was/were broken.*
- If the active verb is in the **present continuous** tense, you use **am/is/are being** + past participle in the passive voice. For example: *am/is/are washing* → *am/is/are being washed.*
- If the active verb is in the **present perfect** tense, you use **has/have been** + past participle in the passive voice. For example: *has/have used* → *has/have been used.*
- If the active verb follows a **modal verb**, you use **modal verb + be** + past participle in the passive voice. For example: *will judge* → *will be judged; can see* → *can be seen.*

 ISBN 978-81-8477-752-9

- You cannot make an intransitive verb passive, because it has no object. The active sentences "*Dogs bark*" and "*I ran to the bus stop,*" for example, cannot be made passive, because the verbs **bark** and **run** are intransitive.

C ***Fill in the blanks with the missing active or passive forms of the verbs, using the third person singular form in each case.***

ACTIVE	PASSIVE	ACTIVE	PASSIVE
invites	____________	rode	____________
____________	is being helped	____________	must be sent
____________	was needed	is cutting	____________
can carry	____________	has given	____________
has used	____________	____________	is said
____________	is opened	will forget	____________
____________	should be treated	____________	has been taken
played	____________	____________	is being done
____________	has been sold	drinks	____________
is moving	____________	____________	was shown

D1. ***Change these sentences from passive to active.***

1. The paintings have been bought by an American art collector.

   ____

2. Protective clothing is worn by all the workers.

   ____

3. Everyone will be shocked by this news.

   ____

4. The prizes were presented by a former student.

   ____

 ISBN 978-81-8477-752-9

5. All our friends are being invited to our wedding.

____

6. A new president has been elected by the people.

____

7. Our house is being decorated by one of Dad's friends.

____

8. Were any mistakes made?

____

9. The word "accelerate' is spelt with two c's and one l.

____

10. He should be warned about the risks.

____

D2. ***Five of these sentences can be changed from active to passive, and five cannot. Put a tick by those that can, then rewrite them in the passive voice on the lines below.***

1. The police car stopped outside our house.
2. Someone has stolen Peter's bike.
3. A caterpillar turns into a butterfly.
4. He slept soundly for several hours.
5. Lightning struck the tower.
6. The children's mother makes all their clothes.
7. Jane was standing by the window.
8. You can recycle most of this packaging.
9. The leaves have fallen from the trees.
10. They heard a strange wailing sound.

____

____

____

 ISBN 978-81-8477-752-9

____

____

Grammar Help

- You can use the passive voice if the action itself, or the person or thing that receives it, is more important than the person or thing that performs it. For example, you would say, "*The president has been assassinated by one of his servants*" rather than "*A servant has assassinated the president.*"
- You also use the passive voice if the doer of the action is not known. For example: *The house was built in the 16th century.*

E ***Using the given verbs, write five passive sentences in which the action is more important than the doer of the action.***

1. ____________________ has been robbed ____________________.
2. ____________________ was founded ____________________.
3. ____________________ must be accompanied ____________________.
4. ____________________ are being treated ____________________.
5. ____________________ is located ____________________.

F ***Underline the passive verbs and circle the active verbs in this advertisement for the Grand Hotel.***

The Grand Hotel stands in the centre of the town. It was built in the mid-20th century and is owned by the Stevenson family. They bought it from the original owner, who also designed the magnificent building.

The hotel is famous for its restaurant. All the food is freshly prepared from high-quality ingredients. It is cooked on the premises by the chef and his

 ISBN 978-81-8477-752-9

skilled assistants. They make a great effort to use local produce whenever possible.

The hotel has 40 rooms on three floors. Guests are provided with everything they need for a comfortable night's sleep, and a team of hard-working staff clean the rooms thoroughly every day.

There is a large conference room on the top floor, which is used by local companies for important meetings. It has seating for up to 100 people and state-of-the-art facilities for computer presentations.

You will find further information on our website at www.grandhotelrivermouth.com. Alternatively, you can call us on 01-344-7862.

Now write six sentences about the Grand Hotel, changing active verbs to passive and passive verbs to active (three of each).

For example:

The Stevenson family own the Grand Hotel.

The magnificent building was designed by the original owner.

1. ______________________________
2. ______________________________
3. ______________________________
4. ______________________________
5. ______________________________
6. ______________________________

 ISBN 978-81-8477-752-9

G ***Answer these questions with a sentence in the passive voice. The answer may or may not use the same verb as the question. The first one has been done to help you.***

1. Who wrote this play? It was written by William Shakespeare.
2. How often should I water these plants? ____________
3. Is there any food left? ____________
4. What is this cloth for? ____________
5. Where is your computer? ____________
6. What happened to the injured survivors? ____________
7. Who betrayed the spy? ____________
8. When will we find out who won? ____________
9. Where did the thief hide the jewels? ____________
10. Has anyone seen Mary lately? ____________

 ISBN 978-81-8477-752-9

21 Direct and Indirect Speech

Grammar Help

- When you write **direct speech**, you put the exact words that someone says inside quotation marks. You put the saying verb outside the quotation marks, at the beginning or end of the sentence. For example: *"What are you doing?" asked Joe. Sally replied, "I'm trying to fix the computer."*
- When the saying verb comes at the beginning, you put a comma after it. You put a full stop (or question mark or exclamation mark) at the end of the spoken words, before the closing quotation mark. For example: *He said, "You are late." She cried, "Help!"* Notice that the spoken words begin with a capital letter.
- When the saying verb comes at the end, you put a comma (or question mark or exclamation mark) at the end of the spoken words, before the closing quotation mark. For example: *"You are late," he said. "Is it raining?" she asked.*
- If the subject of the saying verb is not a pronoun, you often put it after the verb when it follows the spoken words. For example: *"You are late,"* ***said the teacher****. "Is it raining?"* ***asked Jane.*** This is called **inverting** the subject and verb.
- You can also put the saying verb in the middle of the sentence. For example: *"Our new house,"* ***said Peter****, "is much bigger than our old one."* Notice that the second part of the spoken words does not begin with a capital letter.

A1. ***Rewrite these sentences, moving the saying verb to the end. You should invert the subject and verb wherever it is correct to do so.***

1. Paul said, "Please show me what to do."

   ____

2. I asked, "What time is it?"

   ____

3. "This building," said the tour guide, "used to be the emperor's palace."

   ____

 ISBN 978-81-8477-752-9

4. The woman shouted, "Get out of the way!"

____

5. "We have no money," they explained, "and nowhere to live."

____

6. He replied, "My name is Jack."

____

A2. ***Rewrite these sentences, moving the saying verb to the beginning.***

1. "I feel sick," whispered Alice.

____

2. "Why didn't you tell me," asked Mrs Lee, "that you were allergic to peanuts?"

____

3. "This is my favourite film," I said.

____

4. "The thief climbed in," said the policeman, "through the open window."

____

5. "Your hair looks nice today," he remarked.

____

6. "What a mess!" exclaimed Mum.

____

B ***Fill in the blanks with the saying verbs from the box.***

added	complained	cried	declared	objected
replied	suggested	sighed	wailed	whispered

1. "We could go by bus instead," ______________ Anna.
2. "I don't know," he ______________ .
3. The president ______________, "Friday will be a public holiday."

 ISBN 978-81-8477-752-9

4. "Our tour guide doesn't explain things properly," ________________ Joe.
5. "Anyway, it's too late now," she ________________.
6. "I wish we had more money," ________________ Dad.
7. Paul ________________, "I have already done more than my fair share of the work."
8. "Oh no! I've broken my necklace," ________________ the girl.
9. The man ________________, "The house is on fire!"
10. "It's a secret," ________________ Jane.

C ***Write a sentence containing direct speech for each of the following situations. The first one has been done as an example.***

1. You think you have been treated unfairly.

   "That's not fair," I complained.

2. Sally has arrived late.

   ____

3. Tom has drunk his milk but he is still thirsty.

   ____

4. Your father is cross because you are playing your radio too loud.

   ____

5. The greengrocer has sold all his melons.

   ____

6. Your friend is wearing a dress you haven't seen before.

   ____

Grammar Help

- When you write **indirect speech**, you do not use quotation marks and you usually do not give the person's exact words. The saying verb always comes at the beginning. For example: *Joe asked Sally what she was doing. Sally said she was trying to fix the computer.*
- When you change direct speech to indirect speech, you often have to make some changes. When the saying verb is in the past tense, you

 ISBN 978-81-8477-752-9

change the tense of the verb in the reported words from present to past. For example: *Jane said, "The phone **is** ringing."* –> *Jane said the phone **was** ringing. "The crops **need** rain," said the farmer.* –> *The farmer said the crops **needed** rain.*

- You change **can** to **could** and **will** (or **shall**) to **should** in the reported words. For example: *I said, "I **can** see the ship."* –> *I said I **could** see the ship. "Tom **will** help," said Mum.* –> *Mum said Tom **would** help.*
- If the spoken words contain a verb in the simple past tense, you change it into the past perfect tense. For example: *He said, "It **rained** all day."* –> *He said it **had rained** all day. "Mary **was** glad to hear the good news," she said.* –> *She said Mary **had been** glad to hear the good news.*
- You also have to change some pronouns and determiners. For example: *Paul said, "**I** feel sick."* –> *Paul said **he** felt sick. She said, "**I** have lost **my** key."* –> *She said **she** had lost **her** key.*
- You sometimes have to change other words, such as **here** –> **there**, **yesterday** –> **the day before**, **today** –> **that day**, **tomorrow** –> **the following day**. For example: *The boy said, "I live **here**."* –> *The boy said he lived **there**. Sally said, "I will tidy my room **this afternoon**."* –> *Sally said she would tidy her room **that afternoon**.*
- You sometimes put **that** after the saying verb in indirect speech. For example: *She said **that** she had lost her key. They announced **that** they were getting married. The man complained **that** his soup was cold.*
- When you write an **indirect question**, you do not invert the subject and verb and you do not put a question mark at the end. For example: *Bill asked, "How heavy is the box?"* –> *Bill asked how heavy the box was.*
- If the direct question does not begin with a question word, you add **if** or **whether** to the indirect question. For example: *Sue asked, "Is lunch ready?"* –> *Sue asked **whether** lunch was ready. "Can I borrow your pen," he asked.* –> *He asked **if** he could borrow my pen.*

D1. ***Change these sentences from direct speech to indirect speech.***

1. "I don't need any help," said Mary.

____

2. Joe asked, "Why is the door locked?"

____

3. "The man stole my handbag," she said.

____

 ISBN 978-81-8477-752-9

4. "Does your leg hurt?" the doctor asked me.

___

5. "I will mend your bike tomorrow," promised Dad.

___

6. The girl boasted, "I can run faster than anyone else in my class."

___

D2. ***Change these sentences from indirect speech to direct speech. Put the saying verb at the end of the new sentence.***

1. I complained that my soup was cold.

___

2. Alan admitted that he had caused the accident.

___

3. She asked whether I liked her new jeans.

___

4. He said he wanted to stay there.

___

5. The man asked how old our house was.

___

6. Mrs Lee said it was her wedding anniversary that day.

___

 ISBN 978-81-8477-752-9

Unit 1: Singular and Plural Nouns

A
1. boxes 2. parties 3. plates
4. days 5. lives 6. actresses
7. loaves 8. paths 9. trees
10. tomatoes

B
1. These dishes are cracked.
2. There were (some) flies in the soup.
3. Cars are made in factories.
4. The birds are building their nests.
5. Please put the books back on the shelves.
6. The girls made (some) videos to send to their parents.
7. The streets were full of traffic.
8. We bought (some) presents for our friends.
9. The farmers had been ill-treating their donkeys.
10. Dirty, ragged curtains covered the windows.

C

SINGULAR	PLURAL
apparatus	cacti
gymnastics	media
aquarium	cattle
news	phenomena
camera	houses
rabies	varieties
crisis	jeans
taxi	vertebrae
formula	lice
tooth	women

SINGULAR	PLURAL	SINGULAR	PLURAL
cactus	cacti	medium	media
X	cattle	phenomenon	phenomena
house	houses	variety	varieties
X	jeans	vertebra	vertebrae
louse	lice	woman	women

D There were a number of **people** enjoying the sunshine in the park. Some **children** were playing on the **swings**, watched by their **mothers** and **fathers** (*or* **fathers** and **mothers**). Two **men** were sitting by the lake, with fishing **rods** in their **hands**. However, they had not yet caught any **fish**. A little girl with bare **feet** was paddling in the shallow water at the edge of the lake. She had a bag of **crumbs**, which she was throwing to the **birds**. There were several noisy **geese** and a pair of **swans** swimming gracefully along. The formal **gardens** on the other side of the park were looking beautiful. They contained many different **plants** with colourful **flowers** and **leaves** (*or* **leaves** and **flowers**). A team of **gardeners** kept everything neat and tidy: there were no **weeds** to be seen anywhere.

E

SINGULAR	PLURAL
benchmark	benchmarks
break-in	break-ins
classroom	classrooms
hair-dryer	hair-dryers
oil painting	oil paintings
photo album	photo albums
post office	post offices
runner-up	runners-up
screwdriver	screwdrivers
wine bottle	wine bottles

Possible answers:
1. The syllabus sets out a number of benchmarks for students.
2. There have been three break-ins at the store in recent months.
3. All the classrooms will be redecorated during the vacation.
4. This shop does not sell hair-dryers.
5. There are more oil paintings on the second floor of the gallery.
6. Where does your mother keep her photo albums?
7. Some rural post offices may have to close.
8. Each of the runners-up was given a small prize.
9. None of the screwdrivers was the right size.
10. They always put their empty wine bottles in the recycling bin.

F A deadly epidemic is sweeping the country. Several members of my family have had the disease: my sister, one of my son-in-laws and two of my grandchilds. Fortunately they have all recovered, but many others have not been so lucky. Persons listen to their radioes all day, anxious to find out if their lifes are at risk. The news are not good. The disease is caused by a bacteria that is resistant to all known antibiotics. It affects not only human beings, but also animals, especially cattle, which is an important source of income for many farmers. They cannot afford to lose their livestocks, or to fall ill themselves, so they are taking precaution to avoid carrying the germs from their fields into their houses on their foots or clothings. Scientists are working night and day to find a cure for the disease, or a vaccine that will control its spread. So far they have been unsuccessful.

sons-in-law grandchildren People radios lives is bacterium are livestock precautions feet clothing

Unit 2: Possessives

A
1. The road's surface is uneven.
2. Today is my parents' wedding anniversary.
3. Jenny's mother is a doctor.
4. Birds eat the bush's berries.
5. The dress's bodice is torn.
6. The queen needed her lady-in-waiting's help.
7. I cannot find the box's lid.
8. The class's teacher is sick.
9. Sam gathered the geese's eggs.
10. My sister goes to a girls' school.

B
2. men's hats
3. the disease's name
4. a bus's passengers
5. my brother-in-law's job
6. a few minutes' rest
7. James's friends
8. a boat's oars
9. bats' wings
10. a week's holiday

C *Possible answers:*

The dog's bowl is in the kitchen.

Paul and Bill's parents are doctors.

I borrowed a passer-by's mobile phone and called my mother.

Can you read that bus's number?

The workmen's radio was distracting the students.

He was sentenced to five years' imprisonment.

She cleaned out the horses' stable.

The waitresses' uniforms are very smart.

What is the name of France's president?

I do not know Uncle Jack and Aunt Mary's address.

D
2. They are theirs.
3. They are his.
4. They are ours.
5. It is yours.
6. It is ours.
7. It is his.
8. It is mine.
9. They are theirs.
10. They are hers.

E my, Her, her, Their, my, ours, hers, our, mine, theirs, my, his, My, its, yours, your

F
1. There are two **pianos** in the hall.
2. Please give me **your** phone number.
3. The shop does not sell **women's** shoes.
4. This is **my** favourite film.
5. The **twins'** birthday is on the same day as my **mother's**.
6. The patient had a good **night's** sleep.
7. I lost my pen so Mary lent me one of **hers**.
8. The cat has eaten its dinner and now **it's** licking **its** paws.
9. Tom and Peter said the book was **theirs**.
10. Your sisters' husbands are your **brothers-in-law**.

 ISBN 978-81-8477-752-9

11. Are you going to **Nick** and **Sue's** wedding?
12. He went to a **boys'** school where no students ever failed their **exams**.

Unit 3: Indefinite Pronouns

A
1. everyone 2. something
3. someone 4. Everyone
5. everything 6. someone
7. Something 8. everything
9. someone 10. everything
11. everyone 12. something

B
1. The doctor could find nothing wrong with the man.
2. She spoke to no one.
3. I have nothing suitable to wear.
4. Will no one help us?
5. He has done nothing all morning.
6. Tell no one your secret password.
7. Is there nothing we can do?
8. Does no one care about these people?
9. They have had nothing to eat.
10. I sent no one a postcard.

C
2. Did they notice anything unusual?
3. Does anyone know where she is hiding?
4. Was there anything in the cupboard?
5. Did he tell anyone what he had seen?
6. Have they given her anything to drink?
7. Did anyone offer to help?
8. Is anything wrong with this computer?
9. Have the police arrested anyone?
10. Had anything changed in the village?

D
1. their 2. themselves
3. theirs
4. their 5. they
6. themselves … them
7. they 8. them their
9. theirs 10. them

E everyone, someone, anything, anyone, No one, something, nothing, everything

Possible answers:

Did you see anyone you knew at the party?

I went to the market but I didn't buy anything.

Tell everyone to wait outside.

Everything in the shop is too expensive.

No one understood what I was trying to say.

She has done nothing but complain all day.

An architect is someone who designs buildings.

We need something to cut the rope with.

Unit 4: Question Words

A Why, Who, When, how, Where, How, what, Whose, Which, Where

B
2. Where will they stay?
3. When is the wedding?
4. Who (*or* whom) does she look like?
5. Why must the door be locked?
6. How is the patient feeling?

C *Possible answers:*
1. How long did the journey take?
2. Where are you going?
3. Who baked this cake?
4. What time is it?
5. When was the house built?
6. Whose bedroom is this?
7. Where is the milk?
8. Which is my drink?
9. Why is Joe upset?
10. How do you open the window?

D
1. OV 2. S 3. OP
4. S 5. OV 6. OP
7. S 8. OP 9. S
10. OV

E
1. Whose 2. whom 3. Who
4. Who(m) 5. Whose 6. Who
7. Whose 8. whom 9. Who
10. Who(m)

F *Possible answers:*
1. **What** books have you read lately? I've read two books by Jacqueline Wilson.
   Which books are for sale? The ones in the window.
2. **Which** tools should I use? Use this spanner and that screwdriver.
   What tools do we need, and where can we buy them? We need a hammer and some nails, which we can buy at the hardware store.
3. **Which** animals are you drawing? The monkeys in the cage over there.
   What animals do they have on their farm? They have sheep, goats and horses.
4. **What** colour shall I paint the walls? Yellow would look nice.
   Which colour looks best: red or blue? Red.
5. **Which** time is the most convenient? Twelve o'clock would be best.
   What time does the bus leave? Half past five.
6. **What** countries have you visited? I've been to India, Thailand and England.
   Which countries lie next to Pakistan? India, Afghanistan, Iran and China.
7. **What** picture shall I paint? Paint a portrait of yourself.
   Which picture did you paint? The one of the ship at sea.
8. **Which** words do you not understand? "Synthetic", "potential" and 'sustainable'.
   What words rhyme with "think"? "Wink", "pink", "ink", "sink" and "rink".

Unit 5: Helping Verbs

A
1. are 2. does 3. am
4. has 5. Do 6. is
7. Have 8. are 9. has
10. does 11. is 12. do
13. have 14. am 15. Are
16. does 17. has 18. is
19. do 20. have

B

Shop assistant:	Good morning. **Can** I help you?
Tom:	I hope so. I **am** looking for a present for my sister. I thought I **might** buy her a pair of gloves, but I **do** not know what size she takes. Perhaps she **would** like a handbag instead.
Shop assistant:	We have some lovely leather handbags here. They **have** just arrived from Italy. But they are rather expensive. How much **were** you planning to spend?
Tom:	I **do** not have a lot of money, but I **may** be able to borrow some more from my father. He **should** be here in a few minutes. I left him trying to park the car.
Tom's father:	Hello, son. I finally managed to find a parking space. What **have** you bought for your sister?
Tom:	Nothing, yet. There is a nice handbag here, but I need another thousand rupees. **Could** you possibly lend me some money?
Tom's father:	No, you **must** learn to spend only what you **can** afford.
Tom:	I was afraid you **would** say that. I **shall** go and look for a cheaper present somewhere else.

C 1. is used 2. will scratch
3. have forgotten 4. must .. break
5. can talk 6. do … build
7. should (*or* will *or* might) cure
8. are grown 9. was washing
10. has found

D *Possible answers:*
2. My little sister can write her name.
3. He should apologize to his friend.
4. The students must work very hard.
5. She might forget to lock the door.
6. We could go to the cinema.

E *Possible answers:*
2. Did you buy it?
3. Where do they live?
4. Does he know how to use it?
5. Did she like them?
6. How does it work?
7. Do you speak French?
8. Does she need any help?
9. Did you tell her?
10. When did you post it?

F 1. My brother is afraid of the dark.
2. I have no idea what you are talking about.
3. Joe does the shopping and Sally cooks the food.
4. We saw a car being made at the factory.
5. These houses have been here for at least fifty years.
6. Do you know why the alarm is ringing?
7. Jane did not do her homework properly.
8. They were having an argument about whose turn it was.
9. Have you had a phone call from Jack?
10. You are not being very helpful.
11. Mr and Mrs Wilson do not have any children.
12. I was watching Dad do the gardening.
13. The man who lives next door is a brain surgeon.
14. Do not be so mean!
15. She did not know what she was going to do.
16. I am learning how to play the guitar.
17. This is the most sensible thing he has ever done.
18. The winner will be given a prize.
19. We were being very careful not to do anything wrong.
20. It is not necessary to have a bath every day.

Unit 6: Modal Verbs

A You should look after your body – it has to last you a lifetime! There are many things you can do to stay fit and healthy. You must eat the right kinds of foods; otherwise you will become ill or overweight. A healthy diet contains plenty of fresh fruit and vegetables, and not too much sugar or fat. This does not mean you must never eat cakes or sweets – life would be very boring with no treats at all!

Exercise is also important. You ought to take a brisk walk several times a week. Busy people might find this rather difficult. However, there may be small ways in which you can alter your routine to include more physical activity. For example, if you travel to school or work by bus, you could get off one stop earlier and walk the rest of the way. Act now to avoid future health problems. Do not say, "I shall change my lifestyle tomorrow" – do it today!

B 1. may 2. should 3. would
4. can 5. must 6. will
7. might 8. Shall 9. could
10. ought 11. could 12. would
13. may 14. ought 15. shall
16. must 17. should 18. will

C *Possible answers:*
2. It might rain.
3. May I have a glass of water?
4. You must not ride your bike in the park.
5. You could wear this dress.
6. Shall I close the window?
7. I hope your mum will soon be well.
8. I suppose I ought to go to the dentist.
9. You should be more careful.
10. I thought I would be late.

D *Possible answers:*
1. I would rather go for a cycle ride.
2. I would rather have a glass of water.
3. I would rather play a computer game.
4. I would rather have a cat or a rabbit.
5. I would rather visit America.
6. I would rather be a nurse.
7. I would rather meet a film star.
8. I would rather live in the city.
9. I would rather watch you ride it.
10. I would rather sit by the window.

E 1. L 2. L 3. M
4. M 5. L 6. M
7. M 8. L. 9. M
10. M

Unit 7: Present and Past Participles

A 1. believing 2. lying
3. modelling 4. galloping
5. grooming 6. spinning
7. destroying 8. forgetting
9. overlapping 10. buzzing
11. pouring 12. relying
13. defending 14. opening
15. inventing 16. going
17. blossoming 18. growing
19. changing 20. occurring

B *Possible answers:*
2. is drying them
3. is having a rest
4. am wrapping it up
5. are living in the city centre
6. is shining
7. is mending it
8. are going to bed
9. are getting off
10. is looking for a job

C 1. standing 2. running
3. burning 4. frightening
5. flying 6. scampering
7. climbing 8. riding
9. quarrelling 10. dying

D hope – hoping – hoped; dress – dressing – dressed; catch – catching – caught; rub – rubbing – rubbed; bury – burying – buried; drink – drinking – drunk; see – seeing – seen; take – taking – taken; die – dying – died; know – knowing – knew; fill – filling – filled; sweep – sweeping – swept; forget – forgetting – forgotten; swim – swimming – swum; have – having – had

E 1. chosen 2. broken 3. fallen
4. covered 5. met 6. written
7. married 8. given 9. brushed
10. drawn

F Jack was sitting in the garden when he heard a strange noise coming from his neighbours' house next door. It was a loud buzzing sound, like the noise made by someone using a power tool. Jack knew that the house was empty. Mr and Mrs Brown, who lived there, were on holiday. They were staying with their relatives in England for several weeks.

Jack went indoors and told his mother about the strange noise. "I have also noticed some odd things lately," she said. "Yesterday I saw a man leaving the house. He was dressed in dirty jeans and an old T-shirt. I wonder if we should phone the police."

Just then, the doorbell rang. Jack opened the door and found the man described by his mother standing on the doorstep. "I am a friend of Mr and Mrs Brown's," he explained. "They have asked me to do some work in their kitchen while they are away. I hope the noise is not disturbing you." "Not at all," said Jack, glad that the mystery had been solved.

 ISBN 978-81-8477-752-9

Unit 8: The Present Perfect Tense

A 1. drawn 2. drunk 3. taken
4. rung 5. stolen 6. done
7. come 8. ridden 9. lain
10. known 11. forgotten 12. given
13. sunk 14. torn 15. driven
16. gone

B has made, has printed, has sent, has lent, has provided, has baked, has covered, has written, has put, have been, have offered, have shared, have paid, has done, have managed

C 1. has lost 2. has stopped
3 has mended (*or* fixed *or* repaired)
4. have finished (*or* done)
5. have seen 6. have robbed
7. has entered 8. have sold
9. has spread 10. have taken
11. has invited (*or* asked)
12. has left 13. has woken
14. have failed 15. have read
16. has marked 17. has started
18. have cut

D 2. I have already opened it.
3. I read it last week.
4. I have just washed them.
5. I fed it an hour ago.
6. I phoned her this morning
7. I have already done it.
8. I took it at eight o'clock.
9. I have just locked it.
10. I posted it yesterday.

E 1. fell 2. have lived
3. ran 4. travelled
5. has seen 6. has beaten
7. went 8. has bought
9. left 10. has broken
11. came 12. has sold
13. has frozen 14. got
15. have begun 16. collapsed

F *Possible answers:*
2. Have you ever travelled by air?
3. Has the train left yet?
4. Have you washed my jeans?
5. Have I shown you my photos?
6. Has Joe finished his lunch?
7. Has the show begun yet?
8. Have the police found the missing girl?
9. Have you ever seen an elephant?
10. Has Dad fixed the computer?
11. Have you had your hair cut?
12. Have you sold your old bike yet?

Unit 9: Degrees of Adjectives

A 1. easier 2. thinnest 3. widest
4. higher 5. curly 6. braver
7. rich 8. hotter 9. nicest
10. happier

B 2. Sally caught the earlier train. (*or* an earlier train than Jane.)
3. My handwriting is the neatest (in the class).
4. This rock is lighter than that one.
5. Tom's hands were cleaner than his face.
6. The ring I chose was the cheapest (in the shop).

C

POSITIVE	COMPARATIVE
difficult	more difficult
sweet	sweeter
careful	more careful
dirty	dirtier
wet	wetter
confident	more confident
good	better
scared	more scared

POSITIVE	SUPERLATIVE
shallow	shallowest
hard	hardest
bad	worst
amazing	most amazing
fine	finest
obvious	most obvious
simple	simplest
adorable	most adorable

D youngest, older, smaller, cleverest, higher, lazier, best, largest, most delicious-looking, most expensive, cheaper, healthier

E as strong as **an ox**
as **pretty** as a picture
as **high** as a kite
as smooth as **silk**
as **quiet** as a mouse
as **clear** as crystal
as black as **coal**
as sharp as **a razor**
as **tough** as leather
as brave as **a lion**
as blind as **a bat**
as **slippery** as an eel
as busy as **a bee**
as cunning as **a fox**
as **dead** as a dodo
as **cold** as ice
as dry as **dust**
as flat as **a pancake**
as **solid** as a rock
as **free** as a bird
as stubborn as **a mule**
as **wise** as an owl
as **sour** as vinegar
as thin as **a rake**
1. as pretty as a picture
2. as flat as a pancake
3. as clear as crystal
4. as cold as ice
5. as quiet as a mouse
6. as busy as a bee
7. as strong as an ox
8. as tough as leather
9. as thin as a rake
10. as black as coal

F *Possible answers:*
1. sugar
2. a hippo in a mud pool
3. a man's unshaven chin
4. thunder
5. a kitten
6. freshly washed linen

G Dr Jackson was a keen collector of fossils. He had travelled all over the world and had found many interesting specimens. There were hundreds of fossils in his collection, and each was unique. They ranged from the tiny remains of sea creatures to huge bones from extinct dinosaurs. Dr Jackson's interest in fossils had begun as a young boy, when he found a perfect ammonite on the beach. Looking more carefully at the rocks and stones around him, he discovered several more. When he returned home he made a case to display his fossils, using an empty box and a square piece of glass that he found in his father's workshop. People used to ask Dr Jackson if he would stop searching when his collection was complete. He said that was impossible, because there was an infinite number of fossils in the world. He would continue searching until he was too old and weak to travel. Unfortunately, on his final trip to Africa, he contracted a fatal illness and died soon after his return.

1. square 2. fatal
3. final 4. impossible
5. empty 6. unique
7. perfect 8. extinct
9. infinite 10. complete

Unit 10: Forming Adjectives from Nouns

A 1. talented 2. foolish
3. complimentary 4. helpful
5 mountainous 6. careless
7. brotherly 8. educational
9. patriotic 10. dirty

B coastal, troublesome, delightful, customary, wheeled, poisonous, hopeless, selfish, friendly, knowledgeable, heroic, stormy

C1. *Possible answers:*
2. triangular; a triangular bandage
3. residential; a residential district
4. pitiful; a pitiful sight
5. victorious; the victorious army
6. juicy; juicy melons
7. majestic; a majestic building
8. humorous; humorous stories
9. natural; the natural world
10. peaceful; a peaceful protest
11. funny; a funny joke
12. spacious; a spacious apartment
13. basic; basic needs
14. wavy; wavy hair
15. adventurous; an adventurous child

 ISBN 978-81-8477-752-9

16. parental; parental care
17. snobbish; a snobbish remark
18. cloudy; the cloudy sky
19. poisonous; poisonous fruit
20. naval; a naval battle

C2. *Possible answers:*

1. James slipped over on the muddy path.
2. You can make a sling from a triangular bandage.
3. The accident happened in a residential district of the town.
4. The half-starved donkey was a pitiful sight.
5. The victorious army marched into the city.
6. This market stall sells juicy melons and other fruit.
7. The museum is a majestic building dating from the 19th century.
8. He writes humorous stories for a magazine.
9. We must do all we can to protect the natural world.
10. Those opposed to the new airport staged a peaceful protest.
11. Tom told us a funny joke.
12. My aunt and uncle live in a spacious apartment
13. They do not have enough money for their basic needs.
14. Jane's sister has dark wavy hair.
15. Billy is an adventurous child who is not afraid of anything.
16. Every child has a right to good parental care.
17. She made a snobbish remark about their appearance.
18. I looked up at the cloudy sky and hoped it would not rain.
19. You will be very ill if you eat the poisonous fruit of this tree.
20. A famous naval battle was fought there in the 18th century.

D sunny, cloudless, rainy, hourly, Needless, leisurely, botanic, recreational, rectangular, wonderful, famous, colourful, traditional, musical, spectacular, acrobatic, muscular, skilful

E *Possible answers:*

2. Put the **soup bowls** on the table.
3. We have received a **wedding invitation** from Sue and Paul.
4. The **bathroom curtains** need washing.
5. I gave Jane a **cookery book** for her birthday.
6. Joe put on his **school uniform**.
7. The **garage door** was locked.
8. I have lost my **train ticket**.
9. There is a **fish market** at the harbour.
10. The seat was covered with **dog hairs**.

Unit 11: Position of Adjectives

A

1. A	2. Pr	3. A
4. Po	5. Pr	6. Pr
7. Po	8. A	9. Pr
10. Po		

B I am having a great time at the adventure camp. Our instructor, whose name is Joe, is a nice man, but he is also rather strict. Yesterday he took us to the forest and gave us a difficult task to do. Working in small groups, we had to build huts using only the materials available, such as branches, dead leaves and mud. Joe said that the huts must be waterproof, but he did not tell us why. We later found out that we would have to sleep in them overnight, and the weather forecast said there might be heavy rain. When our hut was ready, we had to find something suitable to sleep on. I gathered some dry ferns for my bed. They smelt lovely. When I lay down my bed felt quite soft, but the ground below was hard and I did not have a comfortable night. Tomorrow we are going sailing on the lake. I hope we will not have to make the boats!

Attributive: great, nice, difficult, small, dead, heavy, dry, comfortable

Postpositive: available, suitable

Predicative: strict, waterproof, ready, lovely, soft, hard

C *Possible answers:*

1. tick both boxes; The old man sat down for a rest.
2. tick Predic box; The baby is asleep.
3. tick both boxes; The drink tasted very sweet.
4. tick both boxes; Tom felt sad when his parrot died.
5. tick Attrib box; You must obey the school rules.
6. tick both boxes; This is a dangerous road to cross.
7. tick Predic box; The tree is still alive.
8. tick both boxes; There is a narrow path by the river.
9. tick both boxes; The cat's fur is black.
10. tick Attrib box; We have a history lesson this afternoon.

D

1. The water felt cold.
2. Sally has a new computer.
3. The woman seemed rather upset.
4. Who gave you that gold necklace?
5. Wear something smart for your interview.
6. The burglar entered through the open window.
7. Has Mum found her car keys yet?
8. The dinner plates are on the top shelf.
9. The excited children were awake before their parents.
10. Where did you buy that lovely china ornament?

E

2. The mouse has small round eyes.
3. Uncle Jack's voice is loud and deep.
4. We watched a long boring film.
5. The weather was cold, wet and windy.
6. The insect has a black and yellow body.
7. I picked up a small smooth white stone.
8. Her tomato soup is delicious and creamy.
9. Be careful with these fragile glass bowls.
10. Britain has a red, white and blue flag.

Unit 12: Types of Adverbs

A blindly, accidentally, quickly, sleepily, quietly, loudly, thirstily, carefully, suddenly, properly, greedily, deliberately

B

2. Grandma drives very carefully.
3. The chef sliced the meat thinly.
4. It rained heavily yesterday.
5. This train goes slowly.
6. I play the piano well.

C *Possible answers:*

1. I always brush my teeth before I go to bed.
2. Yesterday evening I watched TV.
3. I never tell lies.
4. I usually cycle to school.
5. I will be thirteen next year.
6. I often help Mum with the housework.
7. On Friday I am going to my friend's house for tea.
8. I sometimes make mistakes when I speak English.
9. I am going to the dentist's tomorrow.
10. I learnt to swim several years ago.
11. I rarely see my English relatives.
12. I had a cold last week.

D

1. up, down
2. off, on (*or* on, off)
3. inside, outside
4 away, back
5. upstairs, downstairs
6. out, in
7. above, below (*or* below, above)
8. here, there
9. over, under
10. outdoors, indoors

 ISBN 978-81-8477-752-9

E *Possible answers:*

2. Our new house is considerably larger than our old one.
3. The water is too cold.
4. Dad is slightly older than Mum.
5. Tom is very good at painting.
6. This puzzle is extremely difficult to solve.
7. I am quite sure that I locked the door.
8. The team played exceptionally well.
9. My feet are rather sore.
10. I did reasonably well in the test.

F

Manner:	carelessly, clearly, eagerly, fast, well
Time:	finally, last night, later, still, this afternoon
Frequency:	every week, hourly, once a month, rarely, often
Place:	aboard, back, down, out, somewhere
Degree:	highly, much, slightly, so, very

Unit 13: Position of Adverbs

A

1. M	2. I	3. M
4. E	5. I	6. E
7. M	8. E	9. I
10. M		

B

1. The children were playing happily in the garden.
2. The weather gradually became warmer.
3. He pulled his sister's hair playfully.
4. They hungrily devoured the food.
5. The branches were swaying gracefully in the breeze.
6. Sally dropped the ball deliberately.
7. He reluctantly left the shop without buying anything.
8. I ran hastily to the bus stop.
9. She was secretly hoping that the show would be cancelled.
10. I asked the boys politely to make less noise.

C *Possible answers:*

1. She rarely wears a skirt.
2. We have a science lesson this afternoon.
3. Yesterday it rained all morning.
4. Jane quietly whispered the answer to me.
5. Tom left an hour ago.
6. Sometimes the phone rings in the middle of the night.
7. Dad has never been to England.
8. The man shook his head sadly.
9. They frequently travel abroad.
10. Fortunately we have a spare key.

D If the fire alarm rings, you must leave immediately the building. Walk to the assembly point calmly by the main gate and there wait until a member of staff tells you what to do. Do not panic and run, because you might fall over and hurt yourself.

People ignore sometimes a fire alarm, thinking that it is just being tested, or that it accidentally has been set off. This extremely is foolish. You should assume that always there is a real fire, even if you cannot see any flames or smell any smoke.

Some people have valuable possessions and do not want to behind leave them. They often waste time picking up these things instead of straight going to the exit. Remember that your life is your most valuable possession. Do not throw away it!

If the fire alarm rings, you must leave the building **immediately** [*or put adverb before* leave]. Walk **calmly** to the assembly point by the main gate and wait **there** until a member of staff tells you what to do. Do not panic and run, because you might fall over and hurt yourself.

People **sometimes** ignore a fire alarm [*or put adverb before* People *or after* alarm], thinking that it is just being tested, or that it has been set off **accidentally**. This is **extremely** foolish. You should **always** assume that there is a real fire, even if you cannot see any flames or smell any smoke.

Some people have valuable possessions and do not want to leave them **behind**. They often waste time picking up these things instead of going **straight** to the exit. Remember that your life is your most valuable possession. Do not throw it **away**!

E

1. Tom has only two sisters.
2. The factory makes only cars.
3. Only this bus goes to the station.
4. My finger hurts only when I bend it.
5. Mum only washed the dishes.

Unit 14: Prepositions

A

1. The milk is in the fridge. **P**
2. The horse jumped over the fence. **D**
3. She wore a gold necklace around her neck. **P**
4. Tom fell down the stairs. **D**
5. Mum will drive us to the station. **D**
6. There is a bookstore at the airport. **P**
7. A car drove through the puddle and splashed us. **D**
8. The spilt coffee left a brown stain on the carpet. **P**
9. Dad framed the picture and hung it above the fireplace. **P**
10. The train from Lahore has just arrived. **D**

B

1. since	2. for	3. since
4. until	5. for	6. until
7. since	8. for	9. since
10. until		

C *Possible answers:*

Jane cycled down the hill.

You should not eat too many snacks during the day.

I felt nervous before the exam.

The plane flew over the city.

Tom hid behind the door.

Fallen leaves lay on the ground.

It often snows here in the winter.

They swam across the river.

We waited outside the theatre.

My brother works at the supermarket.

D *Possible answers:*

2. She sat **by** the fire.
   I am reading a book **by** Charles Dickens.
3. This letter is **for** Mum.
   How much did you pay **for** that jacket?
4. Joe was rude **to** me.
   We are going **to** the park.
5. The bus went **past** the cinema without stopping.
   It is ten **past** three.
6. She left **in** a hurry.
   Your clean socks are **in** the airing cupboard.
7. The policeman ran **after** the thief.
   Grandpa usually has a nap **after** lunch.
8. You cannot make bread **without** flour.
   Mr Jones arrived **without** his wife.
9. She put a blanket **over** the sleeping baby.
   People **over** sixty-five receive a pension.
10. There is a bridge **across** the river.
    The horse galloped **across** the field.

E around, in, by, with, aboard, about, on, across, to, along, for, during, up, at, from, off, after, through, until, of

F

1. P	2. A	3. P
4. C	5. A	6. C

Unit 15: Transitional Devices

A

1. because	2. or	3. while
4. although	5. and	6. if
7. before	8. Therefore	9. but
10. until		

 ISBN 978-81-8477-752-9

B
1. The battery was flat. As a result, the car would not start.
2. If you notice anything suspicious, tell the police.
3. I'll make a pot of tea when our guests arrive.
4. The teacher was angry because we were late.
5. Sally got out of bed as soon as her alarm clock went off.
6. Before you leave the building, check that all the windows are shut.
7. She has been unhappy since her grandfather died.
8. I did not have enough money. However, Dad offered to lend me some.
9. There are several reasons why sweets are bad for you. Firstly, they can cause tooth decay.
10. Tom rang his friend's house but no one answered the phone.

C
1. The journey did not take as long **as** we thought it might.
2. There was no lemonade left, **so** I had a drink of water instead.
3. They did not stop running **until** they reached the end of the road.
4. She cannot speak English, **(al)though** she has lived in England for five years.
5. Tom entered the competition **but** he did not win a prize.
6. I finished my homework, **then** I went to bed.

D *Possible answers:*

2. Do not open the door while the vehicle is moving.
3. The weather was awful, the hotel food was inedible, and the flight home was delayed for twelve hours. All in all, the holiday was a disaster.
4. This jumper is more expensive than the one I bought.
5. Some birds, such as penguins, cannot fly.
6. If you tease the cat, it will scratch you.
7. You could look for the information on the internet. Alternatively, you could go to the library.
8. She read the letter, then threw it away.
9. Jane agreed to look after her neighbours' pets, although she is not very fond of animals.
10. I am allergic to milk, so I cannot eat cheese.
11. You may go home now, as there is nothing more to be done.
12. My brother gave me a DVD and my sister gave me a book.

E before, First(ly), but, However, as, Next (*or* Then), or, If, also, Finally, as well as, When (*or* After), and, until

Unit 16: Punctuation and Capitalization

A
Tom: Where are you going**?**
Sue: I'm off to the supermarket**.** Mum has asked me to buy some food for Dad's birthday party tomorrow**.** She wants bread**,** cheese**,** eggs**,** tomatoes**,** cakes and biscuits**.**
Tom: How many people are coming to the party**?**
Sue: I'm not sure**.** I think Mum has invited about fifteen people**:** Grandma**,** Grandpa**,** Aunt Mary**,** Uncle Bill**,** our four cousins and some of Dad's friends**.**
Tom: Does Dad know about the party yet**?**
Sue: No**.** It's still a surprise**.** I hope he'll be pleased**.**
Tom: Hush**!** Here he comes**.** Let's talk about something else**.**

B *Possible answers:*

2. : a cat, a dog, a rabbit and a goldfish.
3. some carrots, a cabbage, some apples and a melon.
4. : a hammer, a screwdriver, a spanner and a chisel.
5. : Mark, John, Paul and Simon.
6. paper, envelopes, pens and pencils.
7. : India, China, Thailand and Sri Lanka.
8. the piano, the guitar, the trumpet and the violin.
9. : lemonade, cola, milk or water?
10. the lounge, the dining room, the kitchen and my bedroom.
11. bus, train, car or bike.
12. : a newsagent's, a butcher's, a baker's and a greengrocer's.

C1. Across: Pacific, April, English, Monday, Peter, July, Thames, Islam, Urdu, Asia

Down: Friday, December, China, Everest, Alice, James, France, Malay, May, Ramadan

C2. *Possible answers:*

The Pacific is an ocean between Asia and America.

April is the fourth month of the year.

English is the main language of Britain, America, Australia and New Zealand.

Monday is the day after Sunday.

Peter is a boy's name.

July is the month before August.

The Thames is a river that flows through London.

Islam is the religion of Muslims.

Urdu is a language spoken in Pakistan.

Asia is a continent that is joined to Europe.

Friday is the day before Saturday.

December is the last month of the year.

China is a large country in Asia.

Everest is the highest mountain in the world.

Alice is a character in two books by Lewis Carroll.

James is a boy's name.

France is a country in Europe.

Malay is a language spoken in some Asian countries.

May is the fifth month of the year.

Ramadan is a month when Muslims fast.

D
1. The Lord of the Rings
2. The Wind in the Willows
3. Harry Potter and the Goblet of Fire
4. Alice's Adventures in Wonderland
5. A Tale of Two Cities
6. Charlie and the Chocolate Factory
7. The Hundred and One Dalmatians
8. The Adventures of Tom Sawyer
9. My Family and Other Animals
10. The Story of Tracy Beaker

E
1. Aunt Mary and **U**ncle Jack have three children: Paul**,** Kate and Lily.
2. "I have**n't** told anyone your secret**,**" said Joe.
3. Do you know where they live**?**
4. I watched a television programme called "One Man and **H**is Dog" at my friend**'**s [*or* friends**'**] house.
5. Paul replied**,** "We're nearly there**.**"
6. "James **a**nd **t**he Giant Peach" is a children**'s** book.
7. The birds **[delete apostrophe]** are building a nest.
8. I asked her where she was going**.**
9. The man was carrying **[delete colon]** a briefcase and an umbrella.
10. The bank **[delete comma]** is at the end of North **S**treet.
11. May I borrow your pen**?**
12. We stayed **[delete comma]** at **t**he Hilton Hotel.

 ISBN 978-81-8477-752-9

Unit 17: Affirmative and Negative Sentences

A 1. N 2. A 3. N
4. N 5. A 6. N
7. A 8. N 9. N
10. A

B not, neither, no-one, no, never, nowhere, Nothing, None

Possible answers:

Neither of these books belongs to me.

We will never go to that restaurant again.

There was no salt in the stew.

None of the students knew the answer.

No-one came to our assistance.

The sun did not shine all week.

I have nothing more to say.

Homeless people have nowhere to live.

C 1. Jane is not Paul's sister.
2. The men did not work very hard.
3. No-one clapped at the end of the show.
4. The newsagent does not sell English newspapers.
5. I cannot run as fast as you.
6. None of my friends like this kind of music.
7. Alice was not wearing her best clothes.
8. There is nothing wrong with this computer.
9. The animals have not been fed.
10. Joe is never rude to his parents.

D 1. Mum was in the kitchen.
2. The soup smelt very nice.
3. They have done something about the problem.
4. The patient is feeling better.
5. Mary knows what to do.
6. The dog will bite you.
7. James always (*or* sometimes) cycles to school.
8. These boots fit me.
9. There are some spelling mistakes in this book.
10. The woman had somewhere else to go.

E 1. The children were not listening to their teacher.
2. We did not see any monkeys at the zoo. (*or* We saw no monkeys ….)
3. These dishes have not been washed properly.
4. I have never travelled in a helicopter.
5. Mary did not invite Sam to her party.
6. They never do anything to help. (*or* They do nothing to help.)
7. The meat must not be eaten raw.
8. I could not find my mobile phone anywhere.
9. There is no need to worry.
10. It does not matter where you sit.

F can't, isn't, doesn't, haven't, hasn't, don't, wasn't, mustn't, didn't, shouldn't

Possible answers:

Those boys aren't in my class.

We couldn't open the door.

I thought she wouldn't mind.

He wasn't feeling very well.

They mightn't be able to come.

Unit 18: Imperative Sentences

A 1. Wipe 2. Mix
3. Write 4. show
5. Give 6. Read
7. Turn 8. be
9. Close, lock 10. Peel, throw

B <u>Put</u> the sugar and butter in a bowl and <u>whisk</u> them together until the mixture is thick and creamy. You will get the best results if you use an electric mixer or food processor. Then <u>add</u> the beaten eggs and flour and <u>mix</u> thoroughly. <u>Pour</u> the mixture into a baking pan and <u>cook</u> it in a preheated oven for twenty minutes. When the cake is ready, it should be slightly brown on the top and firm to the touch.

<u>Remove</u> the cake from the baking pan and <u>leave</u> it to cool. Meanwhile, <u>prepare</u> the filling by chopping up the strawberries and mixing them with the whipped cream. Finally, <u>cut</u> the cake in two across the middle, <u>spread</u> the strawberries and cream on one half then <u>put</u> the other half on top. If you do not intend to serve or eat the cake straight away, you must store it in a cool place.

C 2. Take the bottles to the recycling bin.
3. Don't be frightened.
4. Help yourself to another piece of cake.
5. Please make less noise.
6. Do as you are told.
7. Wear smart clothes for your interview.
8. Do not eat so many sweets.
9. Write your phone number on this piece of paper.
10. Do not ride your bikes (*or* Do not cycle) on the footpath.
11. Please do not touch the exhibits.
12. Put up your hand if you know the answer.
13. Turn left at the crossroads and you will see the hotel on your right.
14. Never tell anyone your secret password.
15. Guess where I'm going tomorrow!

D travel, Walk, go, make, Save, Switch, leave, Use, waste, Take, Recycle, drop, do, Buy, Encourage

E *Possible answers:*
2. Please help me with my homework.
3. Don't touch the wet paint.
4. Please close the window.
5. Don't forget to send me a postcard.
6. Come in and sit down.
7. Go away and leave me alone!
8. Look out!
9. Please turn the volume down.
10. Have a good time!
11. Don't worry!
12. Please lend me your calculator.

F *Possible answers:*
2. If you have toothache, <u>go to the dentist</u>.
3. When you have finished your meal, <u>put your dirty dishes in the dishwasher</u>.
4. If it starts raining, <u>close the window</u>.
5. Before you leave the room, <u>turn out the light</u>.
6. If the milk has gone sour, <u>don't drink it</u>.
7. When the letter arrives, <u>open it at once</u>.
8. If you are too hot, <u>turn the fan on</u>.
9. Before you hand in your essay, <u>check it carefully for mistakes</u>.
10. If the phone rings, <u>don't answer it</u>.
11. After you have washed the towels, <u>hang them on the line to dry</u>.
12. If you don't know how to spell the word, <u>look it up in the dictionary</u>.
13. Before you wrap the gift, <u>remove the price tag</u>.
14. If someone is bullying you at school, <u>tell your teacher or your parents</u>.
15. If the dog scratches at the door, <u>let it in</u>.

Unit 19: Conditional Sentences

A 1. visit, give 2. wins, become
3. hear, speak 4. touch, burn
5. tell, improves 6. is, take
7. pay, does 8. wake, make
9. arrive, miss 10. get, catch

B If you have flu, keep your germs to yourself.

You will be late for school if you don't leave soon.

 ISBN 978-81-8477-752-9

Do not make a statement unless you are sure it is true.

You will not get full marks unless all your answers are correct.

If the torch stops working, change the battery.

You can come with us if you want to.

If you find the stolen necklace, take it to the police station.

I will not be able to read my emails if I cannot access the internet.

You cannot become a doctor unless you are good at science.

Help yourself to a drink if you are thirsty.

C

1. **2**	2. **1**	3. **1**
4. **2**	5. **2**	6. **2**
7. **1**	8. **2**	9. **1**
10. **1**		

D

1. will	2. would	3. would
4. will	5. would	6. would
7. will	8. would	9. will
10. will		

E 1.1. I would have to walk home if I missed the bus.
2. If the volcano erupted, the village would be destroyed.
3. You would feel cooler if you rolled up your sleeves.
4. If no-one watered the plants, they would die.
5. My parents would be angry with me if I failed my exams.

2.1. If you refuse her offer she will be offended.
2. The dog will run away if I leave the gate open.
3. If I win first prize, I will feel very proud.
4. He will go if he can afford the fare.
5. If she finds out the truth, she will be very upset.

F

1. have	2. complained
3. were	4. finds
5. painted	6. is
7. had	8. lost
9. starts	10. waste

G *Possible answers:*
1. I would become a graphic designer.
2. I would go sailing every weekend.
3. I would give generously to charity.
4. I could have a room of my own.
5. I would change many of the country's laws.

Unit 20: Active and Passive Voice

A

1. P	2. A	3. P
4. P	5. A	6. A
7. P	8. A	9. A
10. P		

B

1. given	2. known	3. laid
4. taught	5. led	6. sewn
7. told	8. thrown	9. spread
10. woken.		

C

ACTIVE	PASSIVE
invites	is invited
rode	was ridden
is helping	is being helped
must send	must be sent
needed	was needed
is cutting	is being cut
can carry	can be carried
has given	has been given
has used	has been used
says	is said
opens	is opened
will forget	will be forgotten
should treat	should be treated
has taken	has been taken
played	was played
is doing	is being done
has sold	has been sold
drinks	is drunk
is moving	is being moved
showed	was shown

D1. 1. An American art collector has bought the paintings.
2. All the workers wear protective clothing.
3. This news will shock everyone.
4. A former student presented the prizes.
5. We are inviting all our friends to our wedding.
6. The people have elected a new president.
7. One of Dad's friends is decorating our house.
8. Did anyone make any mistakes?
9. You spell the word "accelerate" with two c's and one l.
10. Someone should warn him about the risks.

D2. *The following should be ticked*: 2, 5, 6, 8, 10.
2. Peter's bike has been stolen.
5. The tower was struck by lightning.
6. All the children's clothes are made by their mother.
8. Most of this packaging can be recycled.
10. A strange wailing sound was heard.

E *Possible answers:*
1. The bank has been robbed for the second time this year.
2. The organisation was founded in 1827 by a former nurse.
3. All children must be accompanied by an adult.
4. The sick passengers are being treated by the ship's doctor.
5. The airport is located on the northern side of the city.

F The Grand Hotel stands in the centre of the town. It was built in the mid-20th century and is owned by the Stevenson family. They bought it from the original owner, who also designed the magnificent building.

The hotel is famous for its restaurant. All the food is freshly prepared from high-quality ingredients. It is cooked on the premises by the chef and his skilled assistants. They make a great effort to use local produce whenever possible.

The hotel has 40 rooms on three floors. Guests are provided with everything they need for a comfortable night's sleep, and a team of hard-working staff clean the rooms thoroughly every day.

There is a large conference room on the top floor, which is used by local companies for important meetings. It has seating for up to 100 people and state-of-the-art facilities for computer presentations.

You will find further information on our website at www.grandhotelrivermouth.com. Alternatively, you can call us on 01-344-7862.

1. The chef and his skilled assistants cook all the food on the premises.
2. A great effort is made to use local produce.
3. The hotel provides guests with everything they need for a comfortable night's sleep.
4. The rooms are cleaned thoroughly every day.
5. Local companies use the conference room for important meetings.
6. Further information will be found on our website.

G *Possible answers:*
2. They should be watered once a week.
3. No, all the food has been eaten.
4. It is used to clean the floor.
5. It is being repaired.
6. They were taken to hospital.
7. He was betrayed by one of his work colleagues.
8. The winners' names will be announced tomorrow.
9. They were hidden in an old boot.
10. No, she has not been seen for several days.

 ISBN 978-81-8477-752-9

Unit 21: Direct and Indirect Speech

A1. 1. "Please show me what to do," said Paul.
2. "What time is it?" I asked.
3. "This building used to be the emperor's palace," said the tour guide.
4. "Get out of the way!" shouted the woman.
5. "We have no money and nowhere to live," they explained.
6. "My name is Jack," he replied.

A2. 1. Alice whispered, "I feel sick."
2. Mrs Lee asked, "Why didn't you tell me that you were allergic to peanuts?"
3. I said, "This is my favourite film."
4. The policeman said, "The thief climbed in through the open window."
5. He remarked, "Your hair looks nice today."
6. Mum exclaimed, "What a mess!"

B

1. suggested	2. replied
3. declared	4. complained
5. added	6. sighed
7. objected	8. wailed
9. cried	10. whispered

C *Possible answers:*
2. "I'm sorry I'm late," said Sally.
3. "May I have another glass of milk?" asked Tom.
4. "Turn the volume down!" shouted Dad.
5. "There are no melons left," said the greengrocer.
6. "Is that a new dress?" I asked.

D1. 1. Mary said (that) she didn't need any help.
2. Joe asked why the door was locked.
3. She said (that) the man had stolen her handbag.
4. The doctor asked me if (or whether) my leg hurt.
5. Dad promised (that) he would mend my bike the following day.
6. The girl boasted that she could run faster than anyone else in her class.

D2. 1. "My soup is cold," I complained.
2. "I caused the accident," admitted Alan.
3. "Do you like my new jeans?" she asked.
4. "I want to stay here," he said.
5. "How old is your house?" asked the man.
6. "It is my wedding anniversary today," said Mrs Lee.

 ISBN 978-81-8477-752-9